A Tour of the English Lakes

In 1769 Thomas Gray (best known for his *Elegy in a Country Churchyard*) made a tour of the English Lakes and recorded it in his journal, which is now accepted as the first example of modern travel writing. He delighted in what he saw and conveys vividly to us the lakes through eighteenth-century eyes. The watercolourist Joseph Farington RA followed in Gray's footsteps a few years later and painted key views of the lakes along the way. These are beautiful in the picturesque tradition and, from a topographical point of view, are remarkably accurate, unlike the landscapes of most artists of the time. Farington's watercolours and Gray's text complement each other perfectly and *A Tour of the English Lakes* enables us to see the Lake District through the eyes of both artist and writer.

The photographs of Joseph Farington's views are by John R Murray.

John R Murray was a publisher until 2002. He is the editor and compiler of *A Gentleman Publisher's Commonplace Book* and *Old Chestnuts Warmed Up: An Anthology of Narrative Verse* and is also the author (and photographer) of *London: Above Eye Level*. He was responsible for the exhibition *Cartoons & Coronets: The Genius of Osbert Lancaster* at the Wallace Collection in 2008.

THOMAS GRAY
Benjamin Wilson
(John Murray Collection)

JOSEPH FARINGTON RA
Henry Hoppner Meyer
after Sir Thomas Lawrence
(Yale Center for British Art)

A Tour of
the English Lakes

WITH THOMAS GRAY
AND JOSEPH FARINGTON RA

John R Murray

Frances Lincoln

To Ginnie
who supported me thoughout the gestation
of this book and helped me track down and
photograph Farington's views.

© Introductory texts & photographs: John R Murray 2011
© Images of Farington drawings: courtesy the Yale Center for British Art, Paul Mellon Collection

Set and formatted by John R Murray
Designed by Octavius Murray

First paperback published 2012

John R Murray
50 Albemarle Street
London W1S 4BD

First published by
Frances Lincoln Limited
4 Torriano Mews
Torriano Avenue
London NW5 2RZ
www.franceslincoln.com

ISBNs
hardback: 978-0-7112-3268-6
paperback: 978-0-7112-3280-8

Printed and bound in China

1 2 3 4 5 6 7 8 9

Contents

Acknowledgements

Special thanks are due to the Yale Center for British Art for their generosity in allowing me to reproduce the Joseph Farington watercolours and sepia sketches from their Farington album and for kindly supplying me with scans of all the images. I would like to thank, in particular, Scott Wilcox, Senior Curator of Prints and Drawings, for his patience in answering my questions and for supplying me with detailed lists of the contents of the album and also with additional material to help me relate the watercolours to the engravings. I am also grateful to Melissa Fournier for arranging for the scanning of the images. It was this enthusiatic support from the Yale Center that has made this book possible.

Jeff Cowton at the Wordsworth Trust somehow survived all my queries as they rained down on him and gave me full access to the extensive Wordsworth Trust archive. He also saved me from falling into some serious potholes and kept me on the strait and narrow. For this he deserves particular gratitude. Helen Dorey, at Sir John Soane's Museum, kindly made available to me the *Farington Diaries* in the latest edition (with Evelyn Newby's outstanding index) and Steffie Coane supported me during my research.

The Victoria and Albert Museum kindly gave me access to the Farington sketchbooks in their collection and allowed me to photograph images for reference. Thanks are due to Sam Read for arranging this for me. The Bodleian Library kindly allowed me to study William Gilpin's manuscript volumes of his Tour through England, 1772, and the correspondence between William Gilpin and William Mason, 1772–97. In addition their map department allowed me to study maps in their collection covering the Lake District at the time of Gray's tour. Thanks are due to the Armitt Library in Ambleside for alerting me to James Clarke's *A Survey of the Lakes,* 1789, with the maps of Thirlmere, Grasmere and Rydal Water that I have used in this book.

Additional thanks are due to the following for help in many different ways: Stephen Hebron for reading my text at several stages and for his invaluable guidance; Charles Nugent for his stimulating ideas regarding the watercolours and engravings; and Michael Jaye for lending me Joseph Farington's personal copy of Gilpin's *Observations on Several Parts of Great Britain particularly the Highlands of Scotland*. I give special thanks to William Roberts for so generously allowing me to use his transcription of Gray's Journal in Part Two.

Finally, I am once again greatly indebted to Grant McIntyre, who came to my rescue and skilfully edited my text of sound-bites, giving it shape and fluency.

This map is taken from Thomas West's *A Guide to the Lakes*, 1784. The lakes visited by Thomas Gray on his tour have been numbered.

1. Ullswater
2. Derwentwater
3. Bassenthwaite Lake
4. Thirlmere
5. Grasmere
6. Rydal Water
7. Windermere

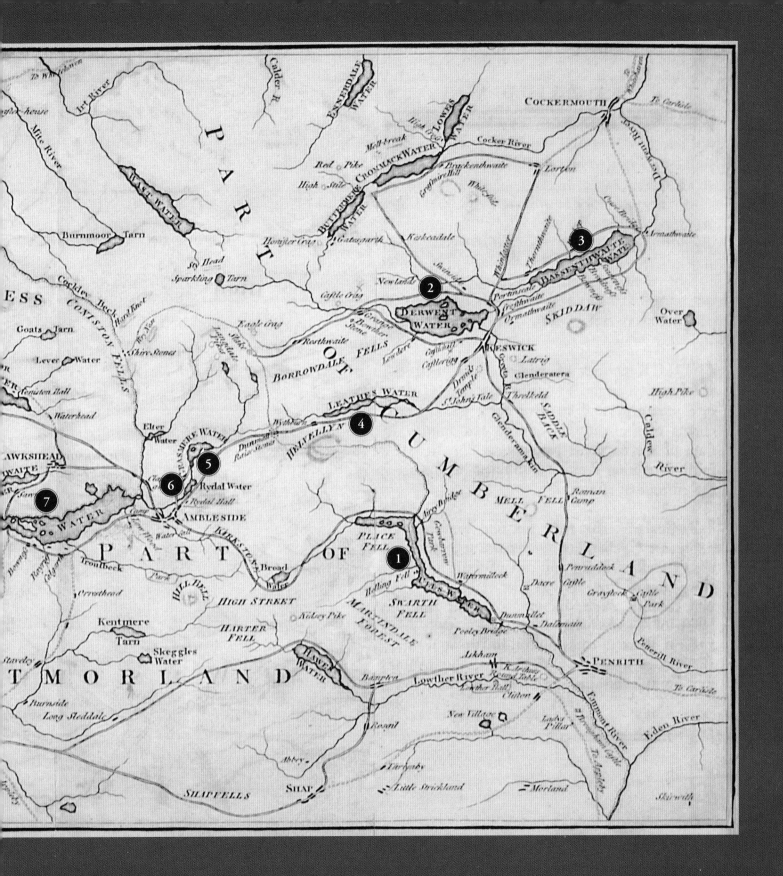

PART ONE

Setting the Scene

Setting the Scene

Thomas Gray has almost been forgotten except perhaps for his *Elegy Written in a Country Churchyard*. He was a Cambridge don, scholarly and rather timid, and he wrote so little that he thought his collected output might be 'mistaken for the works of a flea'. But in his own day his few poems were immensely popular: James Wolfe, commanding the British forces against the French in Canada during the Seven Years War, is said to have remarked, on hearing someone quote a few lines from the *Elegy* before the Battle of the Heights of Abraham, 'Gentlemen I would rather be the author of that poem than take Quebec'. Despite his timidity, Gray was something of a traveller. In his youth he crossed the Alps to Italy with his friend Horace Walpole, quarrelling with him but in due course making it up. Later in life he travelled to the more rugged parts of Britain: Derbyshire, Yorkshire, Scotland and the Lakes. He was in the vanguard of picturesque sensibility, perhaps even a harbinger of Romanticism.

When my father died in 1993, I inherited six small Thomas Gray notebooks, each filled with his tidy handwriting and all housed in an elegant box specially made for them. Something like a resumé of his travels can be seen in the titles of the notebooks. Each one had its contents embossed in gold on its binding, as follows:

> **1.** *France and Italy 1739–1741* [Gray's tour with Horace Walpole]; **2.** *Suffolk 1761, Southampton 1764, Old Park / Hartlepool 1765*; **3.** *London and Kent 1766–1768*; **4.** *Scotland 1765, Bishoprick, Old Park etc., Cumberland 1769*; **5.** *Cumberland, Westmorland, Lancashire and Yorkshire 1769*; **6.** *Mason's Memoranda*.

Having always been a lover of the Lake District (known as the English Lakes until the beginning of the nineteenth century) and having climbed many of the peaks during university vacations, I immediately opened *Cumberland, Westmorland, Lancashire and Yorkshire*. It was Gray's journal of the tour of the lakes he made in 1769. However, this notebook only starts on 6 October at Keswick, though Gray had set out from Brough on 30 September. To find his account of the first few days of his tour I turned to four of the letters he wrote to his friend Dr Thomas Wharton, which include copies of the early journal entries. These were first published in 1775 as part of *The Poems of Mr Gray. To which are prefixed Memoirs of his Life and Writings by W. Mason, MA.* Wharton was to have accompanied Gray but was prevented by illness and Gray was keen to share his experiences with him. I have taken the liberty of adding these entries from the letters to the John Murray manuscript of the journal, setting them out in the same form for the sake of consistency. In this way I have brought together the text of the complete tour.

Gray travelled from Brough, where his arrival coincided with the Brough Hill Fair, one of the oldest cattle fairs in England, via Appleby to Penrith, where he climbed Beacon Hill. From Penrith he continued along the Eeman (Eamont) River, passed Dalemain House (a Georgian mansion looking today much as it did in Gray's time) to Ullswater. He went as far as Watermillock along the west shore of the lake before turning back to Penrith. He then moved on to Keswick, where he stayed at the Queen's Head from 3 to 7 October, using it as a base for excursions. He visited Borrowdale and Grange, passing the famous Lodore Falls on the way. He visited Crow Park and Cockshut Hill and next went along Bassenthwaite Lake (Gray calls it Bassenthwaite Water) to Armathwaite House with its (then) marvellous view up the lake. (This Bassenthwaite part of the tour appears in the Cumberland section of notebook 4.) On 8 October he bade farewell to Keswick and travelled on to Grasmere, Rydal Water, Windermere and then to Kendal and beyond.

I can understand why his journal is generally considered the first example of modern travel writing. It has the freshness and immediacy we value so much today, and Gray's love of the landscape is captivating. To read his journal is 'to come into the company of a warmhearted, good humoured, highly intelligent man, sensitive to place and to people'. Gray was fifty-two when he set out and was as observant as he had ever been.

OCT 1: . . . walk'd over a spungy meadow or two & began to mount this hill thro' a broad & strait green alley among the trees, & with some toil gain'd the summit. From hence saw the Lake [Ullswater] opening [to the south-west] directly at my feet majestic in its calmness, clear & smooth as a blew mirror with winding shores & low points of land cover'd with green inclosures, white farm-houses looking out among the trees, & cattle feeding. The water is almost every where border'd with cultivated lands gently sloping upwards till they reach the feet of the mountains, which rise very rude & aweful with their broken tops on either hand.

OCT 7: Botany might be studied here in perfection at another season because of the great variety of situations & soils all lieing within a small compass. I observed nothing but several curious sorts of lichen, & plenty of gale (*Myrica Gale*) or Dutch myrtle, perfuming the borders of the lake [Derwentwater]. This year the Wadd [graphite] mine has been open'd which is done once in 5 years. It is taken out sometimes in lumps as big as a man's fist, & will undergo no preparation by fire, not being fusible. When it is pure, soft, black, & close-grain'd, it is worth sometimes 30 shillings a pound. The mine lies about a mile up the Fells, near See-wait at the head of Borrodale.

There are no Charr ever taken in these waters, but many in Buttermere-water about Martinmas, which are brought hither & potted. They sow chiefly oats & bigg here, which is but now cut, & still on the ground. There is some hay not yet got in. The rains have done much hurt. Yet observe, the soil is so thin & light, that no day has pass'd, in which I could not walk out with ease, & you know, I am no lover of dirt. Their wheat comes from Cockermouth or Penrith. Fell-mutton is now in season. It grows fat on the mountains, & much resembles venison: excellent Perch (here called Bass) & Pike; & partridge in plenty.

OCT 8: Past a beck near Dunmail-raise, & enter'd Westmoreland a second time. Now begin to see Helm-Crag distinguish'd from its rugged neighbours not so much by its height, as by the strange broken outline of its top, like some gigantic building demolish'd, & the stones that composed it, flung cross each other in wild confusion. Just beyond it opens one of the sweetest landscapes that art ever attempted to imitate. The bosom of the mountains spreading here into a broad bason discovers in the midst Grasmere-water. Its margin is hollow'd into small bays with bold eminences some of rock, some of soft turf, that half conceal, & vary the figure [of] the little lake they command.

Reading passages like these and sharing Gray's love of nature and of landscape, I decided to follow in his footsteps. And, by chance at this same time, I came across a volume of engravings of the lakes 'after drawings by Joseph Farington RA'. This had been published by William Byrne in 1789 with a text in English and French written by William Cookson of Penrith, William Wordsworth's maternal uncle. French was included as many purchasers of engravings were, at this time, to be found in continental Europe, particularly in Paris before the French Revolution and the Napoleonic Wars closed that market.

Joseph Farington is perhaps best known today for his diary, which is full of anecdotes and gives an unrivalled insight into the London art world of his time. But it is with Farington the landscape artist that we are here concerned. He was born in 1747, trained in the studio of the landscape painter Richard Wilson, and became an RA in 1785. Although apprenticed to Wilson, he did not adopt his teacher's idealised landscapes. It is true that Wilson would base his landscapes on those he had actually sketched, but he heightened them through a romantic, Claudean sense of light and colour with elements of the scene exaggerated in order to increase the effect. This was not Farington's style, although he was influenced by Wilson in framing his views in the picturesque fashion with 'shrubs, carefully placed rocks and overarching trees'.

Farington was a great admirer of Gray and an early possessor of the 1775 edition of his writings edited by William Mason, his literary executor and first biographer. This edition printed, for the first time, Gray's account of his lake tour, which contains some of his finest descriptive writing. Farington originally visited Keswick in October 1775 with the idea of painting a series of views specifically to illustrate the tour, but this never came off. Two years later he did travel round the lakes, painting views that Gray would have seen, but he also went to the southern end of Ullswater and further south down Windermere, areas Gray never visited.

Farington was one of the first artists to respond to the new interest in the picturesque and particularly in the lakes, recording their scenery with a view to publishing engravings. The discovery of the 1789 volume gave me another purpose in following Gray's footsteps: I would establish the viewpoint of each print and photograph it as it appears today, almost two hundred and fifty years later. This decision was given yet further impetus when I learned of an album of Farington's original watercolours in the Yale Center for British Art in New Haven, Connecticut. These watercolours, as I later established, were the 'drawings' from which the engravings in the 1789 volume were made. I now decided to combine the watercolours, the engravings, my photographs and Gray's journal into a book.

This idea of illustrating Gray's tour is not new. I recently came upon, in the Bodleian Library, a letter from William Mason sent from York on 13 June 1772 to William Gilpin on the subject of combining illustrations and descriptions: 'I assure you I think they [sketches and descriptions] give the most satisfactory idea that can be, whereas verbal ones are never sufficient for me insomuch that tho' I have Mr Gray's account of the very tour by me at present, I find a constant want of accompanying sketches.' On 23 August 1774, Mason wrote to Gilpin again: 'Mr Gray, who had as much power of words as any man with as much selection also wanted your power of pencil, and I am convinced that they must go together to convey a true idea of the place they are employed to describe.' Mason actually toured the lakes in Cumberland and Westmorland with Gray's journal in hand, and writes: 'It was by comparison on the spot only, that I was able to find out its excellency.' This book in a small way answers Mason's complaint.

*

It was not until the second half of the eighteenth century that travellers began to visit the lakes and write of their experiences. Up till then, mountains had always been avoided as inconvenient barriers to movement. This was understandable as there were few roads through mountainous regions, and those that existed were rough and dangerous, more often than not simply tracks. As Wordsworth writes in a letter to the *Morning Post* in 1844, 'The accomplished Evelyn [John Evelyn 1620–1706], giving an account of his journey from Italy through the Alps, dilates upon the terrible, the melancholy, and the uncomfortable; but, till he comes to the fruitful country in the neighbourhood of Geneva, not a syllable of delight or praise.' Neither did Daniel Defoe nor later Dr Johnson have anything better to say about mountains. Defoe wrote of the lakes in *A Tour Through the Whole Island of Great Britain,* first published 1724–6:

> When we entered at the south part of the county, I began indeed to think of Merionethshire, and the mountains of Snowdon in north Wales, seeing nothing round me, in many places, but impassable hills, whose tops, covered with snow, seemed to tell us all the pleasant part of England was at an end. The great Winander Meer [Windermere], like the Mediterranean Sea, extends on the west for twelve miles or more . . . But notwithstanding the terrible aspect of hills when having passed by Kendal, and descending the frightful mountains, we began to find the flat country show itself; we soon saw that the north and north east part of the county was pleasant, rich, fruitful, and compared to the other parts, populous.

In 1775, six years after Gray's tour, Dr Johnson observed in *A Journey to the Western Islands of Scotland*:

> Of the hills many may be called with Homer's Ida abundant in springs, but . . . they exhibit very little variety; being almost wholly covered with dark heath, and even that seems to be checked in its growth. What is not heath is nakedness, a little diversified by now and then a stream rushing down the steep. An eye accustomed to flowery pastures and waving harvests is astonished and repelled by this wide extent of hopeless sterility.

The Grand Tour introduced mountains in the form of the Alps to rich upper-class travellers, most of whom saw them as an obstacle or looked on them with a fascinated horror stimulated by the dark and awe-inspiring landscape paintings then starting to become fashionable. Salvator Rosa was the best-known painter in this style, celebrated in Horace Walpole's famous comment: 'precipices, mountains, wolves, torrents, rumblings – Salvator Rosa!' But, as so often happens, what first seems terrible later becomes intriguing, and travellers started to look on mountains with new eyes. By the time the Napoleonic Wars had put an end to the Grand Tour and travelling through the Alps, the English taste for mountain scenery was well established. Ahead of the travellers, some early writers had already come to appreciate lakeland scenery. Dr John Brown, who had grown up in Cumberland in the 1750s, described 'the vale and lake of Keswick' in a letter, later published, to the politician and writer Lord Lyttelton (the fifth edition of whose *Dialogues of the Dead* was the first book to be published by John Murray): 'The full perfection of Keswick consists of three circumstances, beauty, horror, and immensity united . . . But to give you a complete idea of these three perfections, as they are joined in Keswick, would require the united powers of Claude, Salvator [Rosa], and Poussin.' Dr John Dalton of Queen's College, Oxford, also originally from Cumberland, wrote in 1755 an influential descriptive poem on the mines of Whitehaven which included a passage 'Enumerating the Beauties of the Lake of Keswick'. His description of Lodore has something of the tone that Gray was to adopt fourteen years later:

> Let other streams rejoice to roar
> Down the rough rocks of dread *Lowdore*,
> Rush raving on with boist'rous sweep,
> And foaming rend the frighted deep.

Gray read and admired both Brown and Dalton, and he became one of the earliest travellers to undertake a tour to the lakes and keep a record of it. In his journal he exudes enthusiasm for the landscape, nature and the life around him. Later, Wordsworth would write that 'the journal of Gray showed how the gloom of ill-health and low spirits had been irradiated by objects, which the Author's powers of mind enabled him to describe with distinctiveness and unaffected simplicity'. This was certainly a compliment coming from Wordsworth, but then Gray's description of his journey up the east side of Derwentwater into Borrowdale is exactly the sort of thing he would have admired most:

> OCT 3: . . . a little further on passing a brook called Borrow-beck we entered Borrowdale. The crags named Lodoor-banks now begin to impend terribly over your way and more terribly, when you hear that three years since an immense mass of rock tumbled at once from the brow, and bar'd all access to the dale (for this is the only road) till they could work their way through it. Luckily no one was passing at the time of this fall but down the side of the mountain and far into the lake lie dispersed the huge fragments of this ruin and in all shapes . . . Soon we came under Gowder-crag, a hill more formidable to the eye and to the apprehension than that of Lodoor, the rocks atop, deep cloven perpendicularly by the rains, hanging loose and nodding forwards, seen just starting from their base in shivers; the whole way down and the road on both sides strew'd with piles of fragments strangely thrown across each other and of dreadful bulk. The place reminds one of those passes in the Alps where the guides tell you to move on with speed and to say nothing lest the agitation of the air loosens the snows above and brings down a mass.

As mentioned, Gray, like some of the early travellers in the lakes, had experience of mountain scenery. He had crossed the Alps from France towards Rome in 1739, a young man out of Cambridge and a companion to Horace Walpole. His description of approaching La Grande Chartreuse in the Dauphiné Alps is a forerunner of his description of approaching Borrowdale.

> The road runs over a mountain, which gives you the first taste of the Alps in its magnificent rudeness, and steep precipices: set out for Echelles on horseback to see the Grande Chartreuse, the way to it up a vast mountain, in many places the road not two yards broad; on one side the rock hanging over you and on the other a monstrous precipice . . . You here meet with all the beauties so savage

and horrid a place can present you with: rocks of various and uncouth figures, cascades pouring down from an immense height out of hanging groves of pine trees, and the solemn sound of the stream that roars below, all concur to form one of the most poetical scenes imaginable.

This is Gray at his most sublime, and writing more than a quarter of a century before his tour of the English Lakes. Some writers criticise Gray's description of Lodore and Borrowdale, claiming he is exaggerating to create effect and that, as Stephen Hebron writes in *Savage Grandeur and Noblest Thoughts: Discovering the Lake District 1750–1820* , 'the passages where he equates the scale and dangers of the lakes with those of the Alps are obviously fanciful'. This may have some truth in it. But one must bear in mind that Gray was of a nervous disposition throughout his life, and also we must read his descriptions through eighteenth-century eyes. There had been recent and serious rock falls before his visit and where roads existed they were narrow and rough; beyond Grange it was impossible to travel by wheeled vehicle. Moreover Gray was not alone in his reaction to mountains. Dr John Brown, who as we have seen appreciated lakeland scenery, wrote a decade or more earlier that 'on the opposite shore [of Derwentwater] you will find rocks and cliffs of stupendous height, hanging broken over the lake in horrible grandeur . . . On these dreadful heights the eagles build their nests; a variety of waterfalls are seen pouring from these summits and tumbling in vast sheets from rock to rock, in rude and terrible magnificence.' In comparison to this, Gray is fairly restrained. And how about Robert Southey (so critical of Gray) many years later, writing about Derwentwater?

> Once more, O Derwent! to thy awful shores
> I come, insatiate of the accustomed sight,
> And listening as the eternal torrent roars . . .

Even today, if you approach Lodore Falls from the north, in early spring before the leaves are out, and follow the track running beside the present road along Derwentwater, it is worth looking up to your left at the sheer rock face towering over you, and observing the vast boulders that have come crashing down over the years and which are now scattered across the ground at your feet. And then further beyond Grange towards Bowder Stone, the sheer rock faces hanging over the road are daunting. You will see that to compare the more dramatic aspects of the lakes with the Alps may not have seemed fanciful in the eighteenth century.

It is true that Thomas West's *A Guide to the Lakes* of 1778 warned his readers against Gray's 'digressions on the dangers of the lakes', but then that book was intended to attract visitors to the area.

West assures his readers that the roads are much improved since Gray's day and Gray himself writes of 'an excellent road' along the foot of Helvellyn. Arthur Young, the agriculturalist who in 1769 toured the lakes studying the 'Present state of Agriculture, Manufactures and Population', made detailed notes on the turnpikes in the North of England and wrote: 'To Keswick – Turnpike very good except a mile over rotten common which is bad.' William Gilpin also refers to the roads in 1776 when he writes: 'Our next undertaking therefore was to ride round the lake [Derwentwater], which we had never done before. It is about eleven miles in circumference. Amusing however as the circuit is, it seems to have been so little frequented, that although we were under the conduct of an inhabitant of the place, we had some difficulty in finding even a bridle road and yet materials are so plentiful, that a little expense might easily make it commodious for wheels. Were the road better, the tour of the lake of Keswick would perhaps be one of the grandest and most beautiful rides in England.' Meanwhile, if the print of Philip James De Loutherbourg's painting *Skiddaw in Cumberland: A Summer's Sunset* (1787) is anything to go by, the roads could still be so hazardous that a coach packed with travellers struggling perilously up a mountain track was likely to turn over at any moment. And James Clarke in the second edition of his *A Survey of the Lakes of Cumberland, Westmorland and Lancashire* of 1789 writes, several years after West, of the road passing by Thirlmere: 'the road lyes under more tremendous mountains here than in any other place; they are laoden [sic] with large loose stones, which seem ready to drop from their sides on the smallest occasion; a sight of sufficient terror to hasten the traveller from the scene.'

*

West's was one of two bestselling guides to the lakes at the end of the eighteenth century. The other, which will be discussed shortly, was the Revd William Gilpin's *Observations on several parts of England, particularly the Mountains and Lakes of Cumberland and Westmoreland, relative chiefly to Picturesque Beauty, made in the year 1772*. Published in two volumes in 1808 . West was a resident of Dalton-in-Furness and a Jesuit priest (interestingly Gilpin was a clergyman). West's guide was the first and the most influential. It was down to earth and practical; it guided the visitor, it did not inspire him. But it attracted visitors to the lakes 'to contemplate, in Alpine scenery, finished in nature's highest tints, the pastoral and rural landscape, exhibited in all their stiles, the soft, the rude, the romantic, and the sublime; and of which perhaps like instances can no where be found assembled in so small a tract of country.' It was very much aimed at artists, whether professional or amateur, pinpointing 'stations' or viewpoints from which the lakes and mountains should be seen to their best advantage. West died in 1779 just after the first edition had appeared, but his *Guide* was revised and enlarged for a second edition in 1780 by William Cockin of Burton-in-Kendal. This second edition included Gray's journal as an addendum, as well as Dr Brown's description of the 'Vale and Lake of Keswick', and the extract 'Enumerating the Beauties of the Lake of Keswick' from Dr Dalton's descriptive poem of 1755. This was the most important collection of writings on the lakes at that period. It was reading copies of these writings by Brown and Dalton, circulated to him before 1755 by friends, that encouraged Gray to visit the lakes.

William Gilpin was very different from West. As we have seen, by the time of Gray's tour, the lakes were already beginning to attract those in search of the picturesque and Gilpin was the first author to tackle the aesthetics of the picturesque and to incorporate these into a guidebook. In his *Essay on Prints* he had defined 'picturesque' as 'a term expressive of that particular kind of beauty which is agreeable in a picture'. He would develop this idea four years later in his *Essays on Picturesque: On Beauty; On Picturesque Travel; and On Landscape Painting* (1792). But in reality he was a practical man, basing his views not on philosophy but on observation. He had little interest in theory and was better writing on the impact of scenery on the sensitive observer, as he does here in 1786 in his volume of *Observations on Cumberland and Westmorland*:

No tame country, however beautiful, can distend the mind like this awful and majestic scenery. The wild sallies of untutored genius often strike the imagination more than the most correct effusions of cultivated parts. Though the eye, might take more pleasure in a view (considered merely in a picturesque light) when a little adorned by the hand of art, yet I much doubt whether such a view would have that strong effect on imagination, as when rough with all its bold irregularities about it – when beauty and deformity, grandeur and horror, mingled together, strike the mind with a thousand opposing ideas, and like chemical infusions produce an effervescence which no harmonious mixtures can produce.

He also encourages artists to compose landscapes as they like them, while laying down firm rules as to what will make the result 'picturesque'. He decides which views are best painted in watercolour, and which drawn in pencil. He stresses that landscapes change depending on time of day, the light and clouds. 'Rocks and woods take different shapes from different directions of light.' 'Under a sullen sky a total change may be produced: distant mountains, and all their beautiful properties may disappear and their place be occupied by dead flat.' However, he points out that 'lake scenery is less subject to change. The broader the features are, the less they will vary. Water which makes the grand part of this kind of scenery, remains unaltered by time: and the rocks and mountains which inviron the lake are as little subject to variation as any of the materials of landscape can be.' This explains why so many of Farington's views can be successfully photographed today and this is what makes following in Gray's and Farington's footsteps so rewarding. However, Gilpin does add, 'Wood is the only feature which can have suffered any considerable change', and it is the trees and woods that pose the main problem to photographing the views today.

It is interesting more generally to set Gilpin's yardsticks against Farington's watercolours. Gilpin discusses how, to achieve the picturesque, views must be manipulated. 'In the body of this book, the author has ventured to call the embellished scene one of the peculiar features of English Landscape.' To him the right balance of art and nature is important. He makes clear that the picturesque often requires 'high colouring' to 'show the effect of a whole'. He examines landscapes by his rules of picturesque beauty and finds that 'nature is always great in design but unequal in composition'. You must first choose the view you want. You can remove any 'deformity' that there may be in it. 'Nothing should be introduced alien to the scene presented.' The only alterations permitted are 'as the nature of the country allows and the beauty of the composition requires'. And he continues:

> Trees he may generally plant, or remove at pleasure. If a withered stump suit the form of his landscape better than a spreading oak, which he finds in nature, he may make the exchange – or he may make it, if he wishes for a spreading oak where he finds a withered trunk. He has no right, we allow, to add a magnificent castle – an impending rock – or a river to adorn his fore-ground. These are new features. But he may certainly break an ill-formed hillock; and shovel the earth about him as he pleases, without offence. He may pull up a piece of awkward paling – he may throw down a cottage – he may even turn the course

of a road or a river, a few yards on this side or that. These trivial alterations may greatly add to the beauty of his composition; yet they interfere not with the truth of the portrait.

For Gilpin imagination and truth had to be carefully balanced. The purpose of the picturesque landscape was somehow to combine the honest and the pleasing, so elements could be adjusted and modified but nothing extraneous introduced. With ideas like these becoming popular, it is not surprising that Claude-glasses came to be used more and more by eighteenth-century artists and travellers to render views picturesque. Mason describes a landscape mirror (Claude glass) as 'a plano-convex mirror, of about four inches in diameter, on a black foil, and bound up like a pocket book'. The viewer had to turn his back to the scene he was admiring and reflect it over his shoulder in the mirror, whose convex nature turned a broad scene into a neat view while the tinted foil (often black or brown) gave the picture 'a satisfying tonal range'. The purpose of the glass was to turn a scene into a picture by reducing and simplifying it.

Both West and Gilpin advocated the use of Claude-glasses, and Gilpin wrote: 'they give the object of nature a soft, mellow tinge like the colouring of an old Master'. Gray carried 'a glass' on his tour and called the result 'a picture in the glass'. On 2 October he writes: 'fell down on my back across a dirty lane with my glass open in one hand, but broke only my knuckles'. But though he enjoyed using it, it did not restrict him from using his own eyes to look and appreciate the world about him.

Does Farington subscribe to the picturesque? When one compares his landscapes with photographs of the same places today, 'embellished scenes' seem not his style at all. But Gilpin writes 'Mr Farington's prints render any other "portraits" [accurate landscapes] of the lakes unnecessary. They are by far, in the author's opinion, the most accurate and beautiful views of that romantic country which he has seen.' This is strange, as Gilpin also writes: 'It is certainly an error in landscape painting to comprehend too much. It turns a picture into a map.' Clearly in his views Farington rises above this. It seems to me that what he does is to combine two approaches. His foregrounds follow the picturesque formula of framing a view with carefully arranged trees and figures, but his backgrounds are in most cases remarkably exact. It could be said that in his 'View across Windermere from the West Shore looking over Great Island [Belle Isle]' he takes liberties with the island, but in general he rarely 'breaks an ill-formed hillock' or 'shovels the earth about as he pleases'. He may exaggerate the size of mountains but he rarely distorts or romanticises them. For him, unlike so many of the artists of the period, the topographical does take precedence over the picturesque. Farington was active at a time when drawing in watercolour was being taken over by painting in watercolour. The former, with which Farington was closely associated, conveyed information, the latter emotion. The future lay with the objective of the Society of Painters in Water Colour, founded in 1804, which was to gain for painters in watercolour the same recognition that the Royal Academy was giving to painters in oil.

It is striking that in none of Farington's views illustrated here does he try to match Gray's sublime and dramatic descriptions of, say, Lodore or Borrowdale. All his watercolours are quiet and calm. Constable's later view that 'painting is but another word for feeling' is alien to him. But the caption to Braque's painting *A Dish of Fruit* in Kelvingrove Art Gallery in Glasgow, is relevant to him: 'There is nothing difficult in his art, no hidden moral or meaning. If we look he will teach us to see and this after all is the highest fame of a true artist.'

Yet Gray's and Farington's ways of viewing the lakes do have a lot in common. They both tend to concentrate on the landscape and not on the people in the landscape. Gray does describe the congregation leaving Sunday service as he passes the little chapel at Wyburn at the south end of Thirlmere, and a young farmer overseeing his reapers in Borrowdale, but he never refers to people who pass him on the road. Farington likewise shows little interest in those who live in the scenes he paints.

One would expect Gray to note the flora of the lakes as, at this time, flora was an absorbing interest of his life. But he mentions only a few such as lichens and gale (Dutch myrtle). As he says, 'botany may be studied here in perfection at another season because of the great variety of situations and soils'. Clearly October is not a good month for plants. Also, although on occasion he specifies oak, ash, birch, holly, spruce and scotch fir, he tends to refer to woods generically. To Gray the landscape is simple, as it is to Farington. Only very rarely, as in his description of the vale of Grasmere where he writes that 'all is peace, rusticity and happy poverty in its neatest most becoming attire', does he get carried away and verge on the tone of the *Elegy*.

Gray's great interest in history is likewise barely reflected in his journal until after Kendal, although he does refer to the 'Druid-Circle of large stones 108 feet in diameter' at Castlerigg outside Keswick, and the traces of a Roman fort on Castle Crag in Borrowdale. This is perhaps because the lakes themselves do not have the castles, great houses or high culture that are to be found in the rest of England. In a way history had by-passed the region. In 1787 a volume was printed entitled *The Travellers Companion in a tour of England and Wales containing a catalogue of the Antiquities, Houses, Parks etc. arranged by the Late Mr Gray.* It is a catalogue compiled by Gray of everything of historical and topographical interest in each county, and in it Gray makes clear his view that the counties of Cumberland and Westmorland, within the bounds of the lakes, have little of historical interest. As Betty A. Schellenberg points out in her article in *Eighteenth-Century Studies* (vol. 44, winter 2011), this work was originally privately printed in 1773 by William Mason, who was the anonymous editor. It was bound with interleaved blank pages for those to whom it was given to check and annotate. The first 'public' edition was printed in 1787 for Kearley of Fleet Street.

Gray and Farington both describe what they see. However, Gray sometimes experiences the sublime whereas Farington remains calm. Neither is seduced by subjectivity like Wordsworth, who was to infuse his poems with subjective feelings. For example, in *The Prelude* he recalls how soothed he is by the Derwent:

> . . . ceaseless music that composed my thoughts
> To more than infant softness, giving me
> Amid fretful dwellings of mankind
> A foretaste, a dim earnest of calm
> That Nature breaths among the hills and groves.

One is reminded of Byron's comment on the lake poets, that the poetry they found in the lakes they had already placed there themselves.

The end of the eighteenth century saw visitors to the lakes increasing, and by the 1790s Keswick had become a centre for 'tourists'. This led to an improvement both in the standard of accommodation in inns and also in the quality of the roads. Visitors became more adventurous and would leave the beaten track to move cross-country and climb Helvellyn, Skiddaw and the other peaks, as Coleridge did when he climbed to the summit of Scafell in 1802. However, it was still an adventure for southerners to go north while the spirit of the Grand Tour continued to lure people across the English Channel to the art and culture of Europe. It was clear that a quite different temperament was required for the lakes.

In the first half of the nineteenth century, Wordsworth's *Guide through the District of the Lakes* became one of the most influential guidebooks. It first appeared anonymously, accompanying a volume of engravings by the Revd Joseph

Wilkinson in 1810, and in 1820 was included as an annexe to his River Duddon sonnets. Only in 1822 was it published on its own. By this time the lakes had been truly discovered and 'tourists' were pouring in. Before long the railway would come to Windermere and another line would run from Penrith to Keswick and Whitehaven, and the *nouveaux riches* would build their mansions round Windermere. The age of Gray and Farington would be left in the distant past.

PART TWO

Thomas Gray's Journal of his Tour of Cumberland, Westmorland, Lancashire and Yorkshire, 1769

The full journal is included here, although part four of this book covers only that section of Gray's tour from Ullswater to Windermere, illustrated by Joseph Farington's watercolours in the Yale album.

NOTE

This transcription of Thomas Gray's journal has been made by William Roberts (*Thomas Gray's Journal of his Visit to the Lake District in October 1769,* edited by William Roberts. Liverpool University Press, 2001) drawing on the manuscript notebooks in the John Murray collection together with the four letters from Gray to Dr Thomas Wharton that cover the early period of the tour. An enormous thank you is due to Bill Roberts for so generously allowing me to benefit from his skilful work.

The text has been lightly edited to make it easier to read. A capital letter has replaced Gray's small letter at the beginning of each sentence. Also Gray's 'w^{ch}' has been spelled out throughout. Where Gray uses 'y^e', the usual 'the' has been adopted. In addition Gray's underlining has been removed as it is not consistent and tends to confuse the reader. Gray's normal inconsistency of spelling including place names has been retained.

Gray confuses the dates at the end of his journal: Oct. 11th should be the 12th, and the 13th should be the 14th. These have been corrected.

Thomas Gray's Journal

Days one to six are taken from Gray's letters to Thomas Wharton

[First letter]

Day One: Brough to Penrith

SEPT 30: Wd at N: W. clouds & sunshine. A mile & ½ from Brough on a hill lay a great army encamp'd. To the left open'd a fine valley with green meadows & hedge-rows, a Gentleman's house peeping forth from a grove of old trees. On a nearer approach appear'd myriads of horses & cattle in the road itself & in all the fields round me, a brisk stream hurrying cross the way, thousands of clean healthy people in their best party-color'd apparel, farmers & their families, Esquires & their daughters, hastening up from the dales & down the fells on every side, glittering in the sun & pressing forward to join the throng: while the dark hills, on many of whose tops the mists were yet hanging, served as a contrast to this gay & moving scene, which continued for near two miles more along the road, and the crowd (coming towards it) reach'd on as far as Appleby.

On the ascent of the hill above Appleby the thick hanging wood & the long reaches of the Eden (rapid, clear, & full as ever) winding below with views of the Castle & Town gave much employment to the mirror: but the sun was wanting & the sky overcast. Oats & barley cut everywhere, but not carried in. Passed Kirby-thore, Sr W. Dalston's house at Acorn-bank, Whinfield-park, Harthornoaks, Countess-pillar, Brougham-Castle, Mr Brown (one of the six clerks) his large new house, cross'd the Eden & the Eimot [Eamont] (pronounce Eeman) with its green vale, & at 3 o'clock dined with Mrs Buchanan at Penrith on trout & partridge. In the afternoon walk'd up the Beacon-hill a mile to the top, saw Whinfield & Lowther-parks, & thro' an opening in the bosom of that cluster of mountains, the Lake of Ulz-water, with the craggy tops of a hundred nameless hills. These to W: & S:, to the N: a great extent of black & dreary plains, to E: Cross-fell just visible thro' mists & vapours hovering round it.

Day Two: Dunmallet and Ullswater

OCT 1: W^d at S: W: a grey autumnal day, air perfectly calm & gentle. Went to see Ulz-water 5 miles distant. Soon left the Keswick-road & turn'd to the left thro' shady lanes along the Vale of Eeman, which runs rapidly on near the way, ripling over the stones. To the right is Delmaine, a large fabrick of pale red stone with 9 windows in front & 7 on the side built by Mr Hassel, behind it a fine lawn surrounded by woods & a long rocky eminence rising over them. A clear & brisk rivulet runs by the house to join the Eeman, whose course is in sight & at a small distance.

Farther on appears Hatton St John, a castle-like old mansion of Mr Huddleston. Approach'd Dunmallert, a fine pointed hill, cover'd with wood planted by old Mr Hassle before-mention'd, who lives always at home & delights in planting. Walk'd over a spungy meadow or two & began to mount this hill thro' a broad & strait green alley among the trees, & with some toil gain'd the summit. From hence saw the Lake opening directly at my feet majestic in its calmness, clear & smooth as a blew mirror with winding shores & low points of land cover'd with green inclosures, white farm-houses looking out among the trees, & cattle feeding. The water is almost every where border'd with cultivated lands gently sloping upwards till they reach the feet of the mountains, which rise very rude & aweful with their broken tops on either hand. Directly in front at better than 3 miles distance Place-Fell, one of the bravest among them, pushes its bold broad breast into the midst of the Lake & forces it to alter its course, forming first a large bay to the left & then bending to the right.

I descended Dunmallert again by a side avenue, that was only not perpendicular, & came to Barton-bridge [now Pooley Bridge] over the Eeman, then walking thro' a path in the wood round the bottom of the hill came forth, where the Eeman issues out of the lake, & continued my way along it's western shore close to the water & generally on a level with it. Saw a cormorant flying over it & fishing.

[Second letter: Oct 1 continued]

The figure of Ulz-water nothing resembles that laid down in our maps: it is 9 miles long, & (at widest) under a mile in breadth. After extending itself 3 m: &

½ in a line to S: W: it turns at the foot of Place-Fell, almost due West, and is here not twice the breadth of the Thames at London. It is soon again interrupted by the roots of Helvellyn, a lofty & very rugged mountain, & spreading again turns off to S: E:, & is lost among the deep recesses of the hills. To this second turning I pursued my way about four miles along its borders beyond a village scatter'd among trees & call'd Water-malloch [Watermillock], in a pleasant grave day, perfectly calm & warm, but without a gleam of sunshine: then the sky seeming to thicken, the valley to grow more desolate, & evening drawing on, I return'd by the way I came to Penrith.

Day Three: Penrith to Keswick

OCT 2: Wd at S: E:, sky clearing, Cross-fell misty, but the outline of the other hills very distinct. Set out at 10 for Keswick by the road we went in 1767 [this was the first attempt that was aborted owing to Wharton's illness]. Saw Greystock-town & castle to the right, which lie only 3 miles (over the Fells) from Ulz-wa-ter. Pass'd through Penradock, & Threlcot [Threlkeld] at the feet of Saddleback, whose furrow'd sides were gilt by the noon-day Sun, while its brow appear'd of a sad purple from the shadow of the clouds, as they sail'd slowly by it. The broad & green valley of Gardies [Guardhouse] and Low-side with a swift stream glittering among the cottages & meadows lay to the left; & the much finer (but narrower) valley of St John's, opening into it: Hill-top the large, tho' low, mansion of the Gaskarths, now a Farm-house, seated on an eminence among woods under a steep fell, was what appear'd the most conspicuous, & beside it a great rock like some antient tower nodding to its fall. Pass'd by the side of Skiddaw & its cub call'd Latter-rig [Latrigg], & saw from an eminence at two miles distance the Vale of Elysium in all its verdure, the sun then playing on the bosom of the lake, & lighting up all the mountains with its lustre.

Dined by two o'clock at the Queen's Head, & then straggled out alone to the Parsonage, fell down on my back across a dirty lane with my glass open in one hand, but broke only my knuckles: stay'd nevertheless, & saw the sun set in all its glory.

Day Four: Borrowdale

OCT 3: Wd at S: E:, a heavenly day. Rose at seven, & walk'd out under the conduct of my Landlord to Borrodale. The grass was cover'd with a hoar-frost, which soon melted, & exhaled in a thin blewish smoke. Crossed the meadows obliquely, catching a diversity of views among the hills over the lake & islands, & changing prospect at every ten paces, left Cockshut, & Castle-hill (which we formerly mounted) behind me, & drew near the foot of Walla-crag, whose bare & rocky brow, cut perpendicularly down above 400 feet, as I guess, awe-fully overlooks the way: Our path here tends to the left, & the ground gently rising, & cover'd with a glade of scattering trees & bushes on the very margin of the water, opens both ways the most delicious view, that my eyes ever beheld. Behind you are the magnificent heights of Walla-crag; opposite lie the thick hanging woods of Ld Egremont, & Newland-valley with green & smiling fields embosom'd in the dark cliffs; to the left the jaws of Borrodale, with that turbu-lent Chaos of mountain behind mountain roll'd in confusion; beneath you, & stretching far away to the right, the shining purity of the Lake, just ruffled by the breeze enough to shew it is alive, reflecting rocks, woods, fields, & inverted tops of mountains, with the white buildings of Keswick, Crosthwait-church, & Skid-daw for a back-ground at distance. Oh Doctor! [Dr Thomas Wharton] I never wish'd more for you; & pray think, how the glass played its part in such a spot, which is called Carf-close-reeds: I chuse to set down these barbarous names, that any body may enquire on the place, & easily find the particular station, that I mean. This scene continues to Barrow-gate, & a little farther, passing a brook called Barrow-beck, we enter'd Borrodale. The crags named Lodoor-banks now begin to impend terribly over your way; & more terribly, when you hear, that three years since an immense mass of rock tumbled at once from the brow, & bar'd all access to the dale (for this is the only road) till they could work their way thro' it. Luckily no one was passing at the time of this fall; but down the side of the mountain & far into the lake lie dispersed the huge fragments of this ruin in all shapes & in all directions. Something farther we turn'd aside into a coppice, ascending a little in front of Lodoor water-fall. The height appears to be about 200 feet, the quantity of water not great, tho' (these three days excepted). It had rain'd daily in the hills for near two months before: but then the stream was nobly broken, leaping from rock to rock, & foaming with fury. On one side a towering crag, that spired up to equal, if not overtop, the neighbouring cliffs (this lay all in shade & darkness) on the other hand a rounder broader projecting hill shag'd with wood & illumined by the sun, which glanced sideways on the upper part of the cataract. The force of the water wearing a deep channel in the ground hurries away to join the lake. We descended again, & pass'd the stream over a rude bridge. Soon after we came under Gowder-crag, a hill more formidable to the eye & to the apprehension than that of Lodoor; the rocks atop, deep-cloven perpendicularly by the rains, hanging loose & nodding forwards, seem just starting from their base in shivers: the whole way down & the road on both sides is strew'd with piles of the fragments strangely thrown across each other & of a dreadful bulk. The place reminds one of those passes in the Alps, where the Guides tell you to move on with speed, & say nothing, lest the agitation of the air should loosen the snows above, & bring down a mass, that would overwhelm a caravan. I took their counsel here and hasten'd on in silence.

Non ragioniam di lor; ma guarda, e passa! ['Let us not speak of them, but look and pass on.' Dante, *The Inferno*, Canto iii. 51]

[Third letter: Oct 3 continued]

The hills here are cloth'd all up their steep sides with oak, ash, birch, holly, &c: some of it has been cut 40 years ago, some within these 8 years, yet all is sprung again green, flourishing, & tall for its age, in a place where no soil appears but the staring rock, & where a man could scarce stand upright.

Met a civil young farmer overseeing his reapers (for it is oat-harvest here) who conducted us to a neat white house in the village of Grange, which is built on a rising ground in the midst of a valley. Round it the mountains form an aweful amphitheatre, & thro' it obliquely runs the Darwent clear as glass, & shewing under its bridge every trout, that passes. Beside the village rises a round eminence of rock cover'd entirely with old trees, & over that more proudly towers Castle-crag, invested also with wood on its sides, & bearing on its naked top some traces of a fort said to be Roman. By the side of this hill, which almost blocks up the way, the valley turns to the left & contracts its dimensions, till there is hardly any road but the rocky bed of the river. The wood of the mountains increases & their summits grow loftier to the eye, & of more fantastic forms: among them appear Eagle's-Cliff, Dove's-nest, Whitedale-pike, &c: celebrated names in the annals of Keswick. The dale opens out about four miles higher till you come to Sea-Whaite (where lies the way mounting the hills to the right, that leads to the Wadd [graphite] mines) all farther access is here barr'd to prying Mortals, only there is a little path winding over the Fells, & for some weeks in the year passable to the Dale's-men; but the Mountains know well, that these innocent people will not reveal the mysteries of their ancient kingdom, the reign of Chaos & old Night [Milton, *Paradise Lost*, i. 543]. Only I learn'd, that this dreadful road dividing again leads one branch to Ravenglas, & the other to Hawkshead.

For me I went no farther than the Farmer's (better than 4 m: from Keswick) at Grange: his Mother & he brought us butter, that Siserah would have jump'd at, tho' not in a lordly dish, bowls of milk, thin oaten-cakes, & ale; & we had carried a cold tongue thither with us. Our Farmer was himself the Man, that last year plunder'd the Eagle's eirie: all the dale are up in arms on such an occasion, for they lose abundance of lambs yearly, not to mention hares, partridge, grous, &c. He was let down from the cliff in ropes to the shelf of rock, on which the nest was built, the people above shouting & hollowing to fright the old birds, which flew screaming round, but did not dare to attack him. He brought off the eaglet (for there is rarely more than one) & an addle egg. The nest was roundish & more than a yard over, made of twigs twisted together. Seldom a year passes but they take the brood or eggs, & sometimes they shoot one, sometimes the other Parent, but the surviver has always found a mate (probably in Ireland) & they breed near the old place. By his description I learn, that this species is the *Erne* (the *Vultur Albicilla* of Linnaeus in his last edition, but in yours *Falco Albicilla*) so consult him & Pennant about it.

Walk'd leisurely home the way we came, but saw a new landscape: the features were the same in part, but many new ones were disclosed by the mid-day Sun, & the tints were entirely changed. Take notice this was the best or perhaps the only day for going up Skiddaw, but I thought it better employ'd: it was perfectly serene, & hot as midsummer.

In the evening walk'd alone down to the Lake by the side of Crow-Park after sunset & saw the solemn colouring of night draw on, the last gleam of sunshine fading away on the hill-tops, the deep serene of the waters, & the long shadows of the mountains thrown across them, till they nearly touch'd the hithermost shore. At distance heard the murmur of many waterfalls not audible in the day-time. Wish'd for the Moon, but she was 'dark to me & silent, hid in her vacant interlunar cave' [Milton, *Samson Agonistes*, 86–9] .

Day Five: Crow Park and Cockshut Hill

OCT 4: Wd E:, clouds & sunshine, & in the course of the day a few drops of rain. Walk'd to Crow-park, now a rough pasture, once a glade of ancient oaks, whose large roots still remain on the ground, but nothing has sprung from them. If one single tree had remain'd, this would have been an unparallel'd spot, & Smith [the landscape painter Thomas Smith] judged right, when he took his print of the Lake from hence, for it is a gentle eminence, not too high, on the very margin of the water & commanding it from end to end, looking full into the gorge of Borodale. I prefer it even to Cockshut-hill, which lies beside it, and to which I walked in the afternoon: it is cover'd with young trees both sown and planted, oak, spruce, scotch-fir, &c: all which thrive wonderfully. There is an easy ascent to the top, & the view far preferable to that on Castle-hill because this is lower & nearer to the Lake: for I find all points, that are much elevated, spoil the beauty of the valley, & make its parts (which are not large) look poor & diminutive. While I was here, a little shower fell, red clouds came marching up the hills from the east, & part of a bright rainbow seem'd to rise along the side of Castle-hill.

From hence I got to the Parsonage a little before Sunset, & saw in my glass a picture, that if I could transmitt to you [Dr Wharton], & fix it in all the softness of its living colours, would fairly sell for a thousand pounds. This is the sweetest scene I can yet discover in point of pastoral beauty. The rest are in a sublimer style.

[Fourth letter]

Day Six: Derwentwater and Castlerigg

OCT 5: W^d N: E: Clouds & sunshine. Walk'd thro' the meadows & corn-fields to the Derwent & crossing it went up How-hill. It looks along Bassinthwaite-water & sees at the same time the course of the river & a part of the Upper-Lake with a full view of Skiddaw. Then I took my way through Portingskall village to the Park, a hill so call'd cover'd entirely with wood: it is all a mass of crumbling slate. Pass'd round its foot between the trees & the edge of the water & came to a Peninsula that juts out into the lake & looks along it both ways. In front rises Walla-Crag, & Castle-hill, the Town, the road to Penrith, Skiddaw & Saddle-back. Returning met a brisk & cold N: Eastern blast, that ruffled all the surface of the lake and made it rise in little waves that broke at the foot of the wood. After dinner walk'd up the Penrith-road 2 miles or more & turning into a corn-field to the right, call'd Castle-Rigg, saw a Druid-Circle of large stones 108 feet in diameter . . .

[The John Murray notebooks take over here]

. . . the largest not 8 feet high, but most of them still erect: they are 50 in number. The valley of Naddle appear'd in sight, and the fells of St. John's, particularly the summits of Catchidecam (called by Camden, Casticand) & Helvellyn said to be as high as Skiddaw, & to rise from a much higher base. A shower came on, & I return'd.

Day Seven: The east side of Bassenthwaite

OCT 6: Wd E:, clouds & sun. Went in a chaise 8 m. along the E. side of Bassinthwaite-water to Ews-bridge. The road in some parts made, in others dangerous for a carriage, narrow, slippery & stony, but no precipices. It runs directly at the foot of Skiddaw, & opposite to Thornthwait-fells, & the brows of Widhope cover'd to the top with wood, opens a very beautiful view down the Lake, which is narrower & longer than that of Keswick, less broke into bays & without islands. At the foot of it a few paces from the brink stands Armathwait, gently sloping upwards with a thick grove of Scotch firs round it, & a large wood behind it. It looks directly up the whole length of the lake almost to Keswick & beyond this a ridge of cultivated hills, on which according to the Keswick-proverb the Sun always shines. A little to the west a stone bridge of 3 arches crosses the Derwent just where it issues from the lake & here I dined at an inn that stands there. Armathwait is a good modern house, not large, of dark-red stone, belonging to Mr Spedding, whose Grandfather was a Steward of old Sr James Lowther, & bought this estate of the Himers. So you must look for Mr Mitchell in some other country. The sky was overcast & the wind cool, so after sauntering a while by the water I came home again. A turnpike is brought from Cockermouth to Ews-bridge 5 miles & is carrying on to Penrith. Several little showers to-day. Said to be snow on Cross-fell.

Day Eight: Crow Park and up the Penrith Road

OCT 7: Market day here. W^d N: E: clouds & sun. Little showers at intervals all day yet walk'd in the morning to Crow-park, & in the evening up Penrith-road. The clouds came rolling up the mountains all round, very unpromising; yet the moon shone at intervals. It was too damp to go towards the lake. Tomorrow mean to bid farewell to Keswick.

Botany might be studied here in perfection at another season because of the great variety of situations & soils all lieing within a small compass. I observed nothing but several curious sorts of lichen, & plenty of gale (*Myrica Gale*) or Dutch myrtle, perfuming the borders of the lake. This year the Wadd mine has been open'd which is done once in 5 years. It is taken out sometimes in lumps as big as a man's fist, & will undergo no preparation by fire, not being fusible. When it is pure, soft, black, & close-grain'd, it is worth sometimes 30 shillings a pound. The mine lies about a mile up the Fells, near See-wait at the head of Borrodale.

There are no Charr ever taken in these waters, but many in Buttermere-water about Martinmas, which are brought hither & potted. They sow chiefly oats & bigg here, which is but now cut, & still on the ground. There is some hay not yet got in. The rains have done much hurt. Yet observe, the soil is so thin & light, that no day has pass'd, in which I could not walk out with ease, & you know, I am no lover of dirt. Their wheat comes from Cockermouth or Penrith. Fell-mutton is now in season. It grows fat on the mountains, & much resembles venison: excellent Perch (here called Bass) & Pike; & partridge in plenty.

Receipt to dress Perch (for Mrs Wharton)

Wash, but neither scale, nor gut them. Broil till they are enough; then pull out the fins, & open them along the back, take out the bone & all the inwards without breaking them. Put in a large lump of butter & salt, clap the sides together, till it melts, & serve very hot. It is excellent. The skin must not be eaten.

Day Nine: Keswick to Kendal by Grasmere

OCT 8: Bid farewell to Keswick & took the Ambleside road in a gloomy morning. W^d. E: & afterwards N: E:. About 2 m: from the town mounted an eminence called Castle-rig, & the sun breaking out discover'd the most beautiful view I have yet seen of the whole valley behind me, the two lakes, the river, & all the mountains. I had almost a mind to have gone back again.

The road in some little patches is not compleated yet, but good country road thro' a few narrow & stony-lanes, very safe in broad day-light. This is the case about Causeway-foot & among Naddle-Fells to Lanewait [Legburthwaite]. The vale you go in has little breadth, the mountains are vast & rocky, the fields little & poor, & the inhabitants are now making hay, [&] see not the sun by two hours in a day so long as at Keswick.

Came to the foot of Helvellyn along which an excellent road is carried, looking down from a little height on Lee's-water (call'd also Thirlmeer, or Wibornwater) & soon descending on its margin. The water looks black from its depth (tho' really clear as glass) & from the gloom of the vast crags, that scowl over it:

It is narrow & about 3 m: long, resembling a river in its course. Little shining torrents hurry down the rocks to join it, but not a bush to overshadow them, or cover their march. All is rock & loose stones up to the very brow, which lies so near your way, that not above half the height of Helvellyn can be seen.

Past by the little Chappel of Wiborn, out of which the Sunday-congregation were then issuing.

Past a beck near Dunmail-raise, & enter'd Westmoreland a second time. Now begin to see Helm-Crag distinguish'd from its rugged neighbours not so much by its height, as by the strange broken outline of its top, like some gigantic building demolish'd, & the stones that composed it, flung cross each other in wild confusion. Just beyond it opens one of the sweetest landscapes, that art ever attempted to imitate. The bosom of the mountains spreading here into a broad bason discovers in the midst Grasmere-water. Its margin is hollow'd into small bays with bold eminences some of rock, some of soft turf, that half conceal, & vary the figure [of] the little lake they command. From the shore a low promontory pushes itself far into the water, & on it stands a white village with the parish-church rising in the midst of it, hanging enclosures, corn-fields, & meadows green as an emerald with their trees & hedges & cattle fill up the whole space from the edge of the water & just opposite to you is a large farmhouse at the bottom of a steep smooth lawn embosom'd in old woods, which climb half-way up the mountain's side, & discover above them a broken line of crags, that crown the scene. Not a single red tile, no flaring Gentleman's house, or garden-walls, break in upon the repose of this little unsuspected paradise, but all is peace, rusticity, & happy poverty in its neatest most becoming attire.

The road winds here over Grasmere-hill, whose rocks soon conceal the water from your sight, yet it is continued along behind them, & contracting itself to a river communicates with Ridale-water, another small lake, but of inferior size & beauty. It seems shallow too, for large patches of reeds appear pretty far within it. Into this vale the road descends. On the opposite banks large & ancient woods mount up the hills, & just to the left of our way stands Rydale-hall, the family seat of Sr Mic: Fleming, but now a farm-house, a large old-fashion'd fabrick surrounded with wood & not much too good for its present destination. Sr Michael is now on his travels, & all this timber far & wide belongs to him. I tremble for it, when he returns. Near the house rises a huge crag call'd Rydale-head, which is said to command a full view of Wynander-mere, & I doubt it not, for within a mile that great Lake is visible even from the road. As to going up the crag one might as well go up Skiddaw.

Came to Ambleside, 18 m: from Keswick meaning to lie there, but on looking into the best bed-chamber dark & damp as a cellar grew delicate, gave up Wynander-mere in despair & resolved I would go on to Kendal directly, 14 m: farther. The road in general fine turnpike, but some parts (about 3 m: in all) not made, yet without danger.

Unexpectedly was well-rewarded for my determination. The afternoon was fine, & the road for full 5 m: runs along the side of Winder-mere with delicious views across it & almost from one end to the other. It is ten miles in length, & at most a mile over, resembling the course of some vast & magnificent river, but no flat marshy grounds, no osier-beds, or patches of scrubby plantation on its banks. At the head two vallies open among the mountains, one that by which we came down, the other Langsledale [Langdale] in which Wreenose [Wrynose] & Hardknott, two great mountains, rise above the rest. From thence the fells visibly sink & soften along its sides, sometimes they run into it (but with a gentle declivity) in their own dark & natural complexion, oftener they are green & cultivated with farms interspersed & round eminences on the border cover'd with trees: towards the South it seem'd to break into larger bays with several islands & a wider extent of cultivation. The way rises continually till at a place call'd Orrest-head it turns to S:E: losing sight of the water.

Pass'd by Ings-Chappel, & Staveley, but I can say no farther, for the dusk of evening coming on I enter'd Kendal almost in the dark, & could distinguish only a shadow of the Castle on a hill & tenter-grounds spread far and wide round the Town, which I mistook for houses. My inn promised sadly having two wooden galleries (like Scotland) in front of it. It was indeed an old ill-contrived house but kept by civil sensible people, so I stay'd two nights with them & fared & slept very comfortably.

Day Ten: Kendal and Sizergh

OCT 9: Wd N: W: clouds & sun. Air mild as summer. All corn off the ground, sky-larks singing aloud (by the way I saw not one at Keswick, perhaps because the place abounds in birds of prey). Went up the Castle-hill. The Town consists chiefly of three nearly parallel streets almost a mile long. Except these all the other houses seem as if they had been dancing a country-dance & were out: there they stand back to back, corner to corner, some up hill, some down without intent or meaning. Along by their side runs a fine brisk stream, over which are 3 stone-bridges. The buildings (a few comfortable houses excepted) are mean, of stone & cover'd with a bad rough-cast. Near the end of the town stands a handsome house of Col: Wilson's, & adjoining to it the Church, a very large Gothick fabrick with a square Tower. It has no particular ornaments but double isles, & at the east-end 4 chappels, or choirs. One of the Pars, another of the Stricklands, the 3rd is the proper choir of the church, & the 4th of the Bellingcams, a family now extinct. There is an altar-tomb of one of them dated 1577 with a flat brass, arms & quarterings & in the window their arms alone, Arg: a hunting-horn, sab: strung Gules. In the Strickland's chappel several modern monuments, & another old altar-tomb, not belonging to the family: on the side of it, a Fess dancetty between 10 Billets (Deincourt?). In the Parr-chappel is a third altar-tomb in the corner, no fig: or inscription, but on the side cut in stone an escutcheon of Roos of Kendal (3 Water-Budgets) quartering Parr (2 bars in a bordure engrail'd). 2dly an escutcheon, Vaire, a Fess (for Marmion). 3dly an escutcheon. three Chevronels braced & a Chief (which I take for Fitzhugh) at the foot is an escutcheon surrounded with the Garter, bearing Roos & Parr quarterly, quartering the other two before-mention'd. I have no books to look in, therefore can not say. Whether this the Ld Parr of Kendal (Queen Catherine's Father) or her Brother, the Marquis of Northampton. It is a Cenotaph for the latter, who was buried at Warwick in 1571. The remains of the Castle are seated on a fine hill on the side of the river opposite to the town. Almost the whole enclosure of the walls remains with 4 towers, 2 square & 2 or 3 round, but their upper part & embattlements are demolished. It is of rough stone & cement, without any ornament or arms, round enclosing a court of like form & surrounded by a mote, nor ever could have been larger than it is, for there are no traces of outworks. There is a good view of the town & river with fertile open valley, thro' which it winds.

After dinner went along the Milthrop-turnpike 4 m: to see the falls (or force) of the river Kent. Came to Siserge (pronounce Siser) & turn'd down a lane to the left. Siser, the seat of the Stricklands an old Catholick family, is an ancient Hall-house, with a very large tower embattled: the rest of the buildings added to this are of later date, but all is white & seen to advantage on a back ground of old trees: there is a small park also well-wooded. Opposite to this turn'd to the left & soon came to the river. It works its way in a narrow & deep rocky channel o'erhung with trees. the calmness & brightness of the evening, the roar of the waters, & the thumping of huge hammers at an iron-forge not far distant made it a singular walk, but as to the falls (for there are two) they are not 4 feet high. I went on down to the forge & saw the Dæmons at work by the light of their own fires: the iron is brought in pigs to Milthrop by sea from Scotland &c. & is here beat into bars & plates. Two miles farther at Levens is the seat of Ld Suffolk, where he sometimes passes the summer. It was a favourite place of his late Countess: but this I did not see.

Day Eleven: Kendal to Lancaster

OCT 10: Went by Burton to Lancaster. Wd N: W: clouds & sun. 22m: very good country well enclosed & wooded with some common interspersed. Pass'd at the foot of Farlton-knot, a high fell. 4 m: N: of Lancaster on a rising ground call'd Bolton (pron: Bouton)-Wait had a full view of Cartmell-sands with here and there a Passenger riding over them (it being low water), the points of Furness shooting far into the sea, & lofty mountains partly cover'd with clouds extending North of them. Lancaster also appear'd very conspicuous & fine, for its most distinguish'd features the Castle & Church, mounted on a green eminence, were all that could be seen. Woe is me! when I got thither, it was the second day of their fair. The Inn (in the principal street) was a great old gloomy house full of people, but I found tolerable quarters, & even slept two nights in peace.

Ascended the Castle-hill in a fine afternoon. It takes up the higher top of the eminence on which it stands, & is irregularly round, encompassed with a deep mote. In front towards the Town is a magnificent Gothick Gateway, lofty & huge, the overhanging battlements are supported by a triple range of corbels, the intervals pierced thro' & shewing the day from above. On its top rise light watchtowers of small height. It opens below with a grand pointed arch: over this is a wrought tabernacle, doubtless once containing the Founder's figure, on one side a shield of France semy quarter'd with England, on the other the same with a label ermine for John of Gaunt D: of Lancaster. This opens to a court within, which I did not much care to enter, being the County Gaol & full of Prisoners, both Criminals & Debtors. From this gateway the walls continue & join it to a vast square tower of great height, the lower part at least of remote antiquity, for it has small round-headed lights with plain short pillars on each side of them, there is a third tower also square & of less dimensions. This is all the castle, near it & but little lower stands the Church, a large & plain Gothic fabrick, the high square Tower at the West-end has been rebuilt of late years, but nearly in the same style. There are no ornaments of arms, &c: anywhere to be seen. Within it is lightsome & spacious, but not one monument of antiquity, or piece of painted glass is left. From the Church-yard there is an extensive sea-view (for now the tide had almost cover'd the sands, & fill'd the river) & besides greatest part of Furness I could distinguish Peel-Castle on the isle of Fowdrey [Foulney], which lies off its southern extremity. The Town is built on the slope & at the feet of Castle-hill more than twice the bigness of Aukland with many neat buildings of white stone, but a little disorderly in their positions ad libitum, like Kendal. many also extend below on the keys by the river-side, where a number of ships were moor'd, some of them three-mast vessels deck'd out with their colours in honor of the Fair. Here is a good bridge of 4 arches over the Lune, which runs (when the tide is out) in two streams divided by a bed of gravel, which is not cover'd but in spring-tides. Below the town it widens to near the breadth of the Thames at London, & meets the sea at 5 or 6 m: distance to S:W.

Day Twelve: Poulton and the Sands

OCT 11: Wd S: W: clouds & sun. Warm & a fine dappled sky. Cross'd the river & walk'd over a peninsula 3 miles to the village of Pooton which stands on the beach. An old Fisherman mending his nets (while I enquired about the danger of passing those sands) told me in his dialect a moving story, how a brother of the trade, a Cockler (as he styled him), driving a little cart with two daughters (women grown) in it, & his Wife on horseback following, set out one day to pass the 7 mile sands, as they had frequently been used to do, for nobody in the village knew them better than the old Man did. When they were about half way over, a thick fog rose, & as they advanced, they found the water much deeper than they expected. The old man was puzzled, he stop'd, & said he would go a little way to find some mark he was acquainted with. They staid a little while for him, but in vain. They call'd aloud, but no reply. At last the young women press'd their mother to think, where they were, & go on. She would not leave the place, she wander'd about forlorn & amazed, she would not quit her horse, & get into the cart with them. They determined after much time wasted to turn back, & give themselves up to the guidance of the horses. The old Woman was soon wash'd off and perish'd. The poor Girls clung close to their cart, & the horse sometimes wading & sometimes swimming brought them back to land alive, but senseless with terror & distress & unable for many days to give any account of themselves. The bodies of their parents were found soon after (next ebb); that of the Father a very few paces distant from the spot, where he had left them.

In the afternoon wander'd about the town & by the key till it grew dark. A little rain fell.

Day Thirteen: Lancaster to Settle

OCT 12: Wd N: E: sky gloomy, then gleams of sunshine. Set out for Settle by a fine turnpike road, 29 miles. Rich & beautiful enclosed country diversified with frequent villages & churches, very unequal ground, & on the left the river Lune winding in a deep valley, its hanging banks clothed with fine woods, thro' which you catch long reaches of the water, as the road winds about at a considerable height above it. Pass'd the Park (Hon: Mr Clifford's, a catholick) in the most picturesque part of the way. The grounds between him & the river are indeed charming: the house is ordinary, & the park nothing but a rocky fell scatter'd over with ancient hawthorns. Came to Hornby a little Town on the river Wenning, over which a handsome bridge is now in building. The Castle in a lordly situation attracted me, so I walk'd up the hill to it. First presents itself a large but ordinary white Gentleman's house sash'd. Behind it rises the ancient Keep built by Edward Stanley, Lord Mounteagle (inscribed Helas et quand?), he died about 1524 in Henry 8th's time. It is now a shell only, tho' rafters are laid within it as for flooring. I went up a winding stone-staircase in one corner to the leads, & at the angle is a single hexagon watch-tower rising some feet higher, fitted up in the tast of a modern Toot with sash-windows in gilt frames, & a stucco cupola, & on the top a vast gilt eagle by Mr Charteris, the present Possessor. But he has not lived here since the year 1745, when the people of Lancaster insulted him, threw stones into his coach, & almost made his wife (Lady Katherine Gordon) miscarry. Since that he has built a great ugly house of red stone (thank God it is not in England) near Haddington, which I remember to have passed by. He is the 2d Son of the Earl of Wemyss, & brother to the Ld Elcho, Grandson to Col: Charteris, whose name he bears.

From the leads of the Tower there is a fine view of the country round, & much wood near the castle. Ingleborough, which I had seen before distinctly at Lancaster to N:E: was now compleatly wrap'd in clouds all but its summit, which might have been easily mistaken for a long black cloud too, fraught with an approaching storm. Now our road begun gradually to mount toward the Apennine, the trees growing less, & thinner of leaves, till we came to Ingleton 18 m: It is a pretty village situated very high & yet in a valley at the foot of that huge creature of God Ingleborough. Two torrents cross it with great stones roll'd along their bed instead of water: over them are two handsome arches flung. Here at a little ale-house were Sr Bellingcam Graham & Mr Parker, L^d of the Manour (one of them 6 feet ½ high, & the other as much in breadth) come to dine.

The nipping air (tho' the afternoon was growing very bright) now taught us, we were in Craven. The road was all up & down (tho' no where very steep). To the left were mountain-tops (Weryside), to the right a wide valley (all inclosed ground) & beyond it high hills again. In approaching Settle the crags on the left drew nearer to our way, till we ascended Brunton-brow, into a chearful valley (tho' thin of trees) to Giggleswick a village with a small piece of water by its side cover'd over with coots. Near it a Church, which belongs also to Settle & half a mile farther having passed the Ribble over a bridge arrived at Settle. It is a small market-town standing directly under a rocky fell. There are not a dozen good-looking houses, the rest are old & low with little wooden portico's in front. My inn pleased me much (tho' small) for the neatness & civility of the good Woman that kept it, so I lay there two nights, & went [to visit Gordale-Scar].

Day Fourteen: Gordale Scar

OCT 13: [From Settle I went] to visit Gordale-Scar. Wd N: E: day gloomy & cold. It lay but 6 m: from Settle, but that way was directly over a Fell, & it might rain, so I went round in a chaise the only way one could get near it in a carriage, which made it full 13 m: & half of it such a road! But I got safe over it, so there's an end, & came to Malham (pronounce Maum) a village in the bosom of the mountains seated in a wild & dreary valley. From thence I was to walk a mile over very rough ground, a torrent rattling along on the left hand. On the cliffs above hung a few goats: one of them danced & scratched an ear with its hind-foot in a place where I would not have stood stock-still, 'for all beneath the moon' [Shakespeare, *King Lear*, iv. 6. 26]. As I advanced the crags seem'd to close in, but discover'd a narrow entrance turning to the left between them. I followed my guide a few paces, & lo, the hills open'd again into no large space, & then all farther way is bar'd by a stream, that at the height of about 50 feet gushes from a hole in the rock, & spreading in large sheets over its broken front dashes from steep to steep, & then rattles away in a torrent down the valley. The rock on the left rises perpendicular with stubbed yew-trees & shrubs, staring from its side to the height of at least 300 feet but these are not the thing! It is that to the right, under which you stand to see the fall, that forms the principal horror of the place. From its very base it begins to slope forwards over you in one black & solid mass without any crevice in its surface, & overshadows half the area below with its dreadful canopy. When I stood at (I believe) full 4 yards distance from its foot, the drops which perpetually distill from its brow, fell on my head, & in one part of its top more exposed to the weather there are loose stones that hang in air, & threaten visibly some idle Spectator with instant destruction. It is safer to shelter yourself close to its bottom, & trust the mercy of that enormous mass, which nothing but an earthquake can stir. The gloomy uncomfortable day well suited the savage aspect of the place, & made it still more formidable. I stay'd there (not without shuddering) a quarter of an hour, & thought my trouble richly paid, for the impression will last for life. At the alehouse where I dined in Malham, Vivares, the landscape-painter, had lodged for a week or more. Smith & Bellers had also been there, & two prints of Gordale have been engraved by them. Return'd to my comfortable inn. Night fine, but windy & frosty.

Day Fifteen: Settle to Otley

Oct 14: Went to Skipton, 16 miles. Wd N: E: gloomy, at one o'clock a little sleet falls. From several parts of the road, & in many places about Settle I saw at once the three famous hills of this country, Ingleborough, Penigent, & Pendle, the first is esteem'd the highest. Their features are hard to describe, but I could trace their outline with a pencil.

Craven after all is an unpleasing country, when seen from a height. Its valleys are chiefly wide & either marshy, or enclosed pasture with a few trees. Numbers of black cattle are fatted here, both of the Scotch breed, & a larger sort of oxen with great horns. There is little cultivated grounds, except a few oats.

W^d N. E. gloomy. At noon a few grains of sleet fell, then bright & clear. Went thro' Long Preston & Gargrave to Skipton 16 miles. It is a pretty large Market-Town in a valley with one very broad street gently sloping downwards from the Castle, which stands at the head of it. This is one of our good Countesse's buildings, but on old foundations: it is not very large, but of a handsome antique appearance with round towers, a grand gateway, bridge & mote, & many old trees about it, in good repair, & kept up, as a habitation of the Earl of Thanet, tho' he rarely comes thither. What with the sleet & a foolish dispute about chaises, that delay'd me, I did not see the inside of it, but went on 15 miles to Ottley. First up Shode-bank, the steepest hill I ever saw a road carried over in England, for it mounts in a strait line (without any other repose for the horses, than by placing stones every now & then behind the wheels) for a full mile. Then the road goes on a level along the brow of this high hill over Rumbald-moor, till it gently descends into Wharfdale: so they call the Vale of the Wharf, & a beautiful vale it is, well-wooded, well-cultivated, well-inhabited, but with high crags at a distance, that border the green country on either hand. Thro' the midst of it deep, clear, full to the brink, & of no inconsiderable breadth runs in long windings the river. How it comes to pass that it should be so fine & copious a stream here, & at Tadcaster (so much lower) should have nothing but a wide stony channel without water, I can not tell you. I pass'd through Long-Addingham, Ilkley (pronounce Eecla) distinguished by a lofty brow of loose rocks to the right, Burley, a neat & pretty village among trees. On the opposite side of the river lay Middleton-Lodge, belonging to a Catholick Gentleman of that name; Weston, a venerable stone fabrick with large offices, of Mr Vavasor, the meadows in front gently descending to the water, & behind a great & shady wood; Farnley (Mr Fawke's) a place like the last, but larger, & rising higher on the side of the hill. Ottley is a large airy Town, with clean but low rustick buildings, & a bridge over the Wharf. I went into its spatious Gothic Church, which has been new-roof'd with a flat stucco ceiling. In a corner of it is the monument of Tho: Ld Fairfax, & Helen Aske, his Lady, descended from the Cliffords & Lattimers, as her epitaph says. The figures not ill-cut particularly his in armour, but bare-headed, lie on the tomb. I take them for the Grand Parents of the famous Sr Tho: Fairfax.

PART THREE

Joseph Farington:
the Watercolours and Engravings

NOTE

Sources of the watercolours, sepia sketches and engravings.

1. The album: in the possession of the Yale Center for British Art, Paul Mellon Collection containing twenty-four watercolour drawings and nineteen sepia sketches by Joseph Farington, RA. These are all reproduced in this book. Although one of the views is outside Gray's tour and one is unidentified, these have been included at the end to give full coverage of the album.

2. *Views of the Lakes etc. in Cumberland and Westmorland. Engraved from drawings made by Joseph Farington R.A.* Published by William Byrne, London 1789. This volume contains twenty full-page engravings, all of which are reproduced in this book. These twenty engravings were originally produced as loose prints in the 1780s before being combined into a single volume in 1789.

3. *The Lakes of Lancashire, Westmorland and Cumberland: Delineated in forty-three engravings from drawings by Joseph Farington R.A. The result of a tour made in the summer of 1816. By Thomas Hartwell Horne.* T. Cadell & W. Davies, Strand. London, 1816. All these prints were engraved in either 1815 or 1816. Only a few of these have been included in this book.

Joseph Farington: the Watercolours and Engravings

Farington's watercolours and ink-and-wash (sepia) sketches relating to Gray's tour are taken from the album in the collection of the Yale Center for British Art and are reproduced alongside the engravings from his drawings which appear in *Views of the Lakes etc. in Cumberland and Westmorland*, published in 1789 with a text by William Cookson. There are also a few engravings from Thomas Hartwell Horne's *The Lakes of Lancashire, Westmorland and Cumberland etc.*, published in 1816. Views taken from this latter volume have been selected as they are relevant to Gray's tour but do not appear in the 1789 volume. In addition I have included present-day photographs, taken whenever possible from Farington's own viewpoints.

Farington was, as we have seen, one of the first serious artists to record the lake scenery with a view to publishing sets of engravings. The process is described by Cockin in his 1784 edition of West's *A Guide to the Lakes* where readers are advised that engravings of Farington's drawings are in preparation:

> Having been of late years much frequented, and it being often suggested by those who have seen them, that views of the most striking features in this part of England would afford entertainment to the lovers of picturesque beauty, it is presumed the following proposal for the publication of six views will meet with approbation. The subjects are as follows: 1 A general view of Derwentwater, and the vale of Keswick, from Ashness. 2. Derwent-water and Skiddaw, from Brandelow-woods. 3. Lowdore water-fall. 4. The Grange in Borrowdale. 5. Grasmere. 6. Rydal-water. Which will be engraved by WILLIAM BYRNE, etc. from the drawings of J. FARINGTON. The size of each plate will be 14½ inches by 10 inches. The pricing to subscribers will be one pound and six shillings; half to be paid at time of subscribing, the remainder on delivery of the prints . . . In selecting these views of the Lakes, one principal endeavour of the artist has been to choose those points where the peculiar distinction of each lake marks itself. In

the vicinity of every lake there are a thousand romantic circumstances calculated for the pencil; but in a limited work, it is supposed it will be most satisfactory to give such subjects as may fix in the memory of those who have visited the lakes and scenes they have viewed, and also afford a general idea of the appearance of the country, to those who may not have been in this part of England.

After the first set is published (which will be about Christmas next) the proprietors mean to proceed with views of *Windermere, Ulls-water,* etc. and the most remarkable features in their neighbourhoods; the drawings of which being already made, the work will be carried on with expedition, as the second set can in part be proceeding while the first set is executing.

The drawings, and such of the prints as are finished, or forwarding, may be seen at *Mr. Byrne's No 79, Titchfield-street, Oxford Road,* where subscriptions are received, as also at *Mr Farington's, Upper Charlotte-street, Rathbone-place.*

Sets of engravings of this kind found a ready market amongst tourists, particularly those confined to Britain by the French Revolution and the Napoleonic wars. This was clearly a way for an artist to make money. One artist friend of Farington who took advantage of this was Thomas Hearne, who produced a series of drawings of historical sites in Great Britain in response to the antiquarian interest steadily growing at that time. They were engraved and appeared as *The Antiquities of Great Britain* in two volumes, the first in 1786 and the second 1806. The engraver William Byrne was once again the publisher.

After I had acquired the 1789 volume of Farington's engravings, I visited the Wordsworth Trust in Grasmere and asked Robert Woof, its then director, if he knew the whereabouts of the original Farington landscapes. He suggested that they might be in the Farington album in the Yale Center for British Art. I wrote to Scott Wilcox, Senior Curator at the Yale Center, asking him for details of the contents of the album. He sent me a most friendly reply enclosing a list of the subjects included. As there were doubts as to whether these were what I was looking for, he invited me to pay a visit to New Haven to look at the album for myself. This I did, and I was delighted to find that the album contained watercolours of all the views appearing in the engravings in the 1789 volume. Finding this album would give my project a whole new dimension.

When I returned home I compared the notes I had made in New Haven with the actual engravings. It was clear that the Yale watercolours were exactly what I needed to accompany them. I then wrote to Yale and asked tentatively if I could be supplied with scans of the watercolours. With enormous generosity Yale arranged for the contents of the entire album (watercolours as well as the pen-and-ink drawings and wash sketches) to be scanned and they sent me a complete set in both high and low resolution, thus making it possible to reproduce the images in this book.

My natural assumption was that the Farington paintings in the Yale album had been used for the engravings in the 1789 volume. But it turned out that the view generally held among experts was that the paintings in fact postdated the engravings. To substantiate this I was referred to the 'note no. 231' in *William Wordworth and the Age of English Romanticism*, the book that accompanied the exhibition of the same name of 1987 held in New York, Chicago and Bloomington. This note is headed 'Grasmere in Album [the Yale Farington album], Lake District Views illustrating Gray's Tour, dated c. 1798'. The date 1798 concerned me, as the volume of engravings is dated 1789 and the views in it were engraved in the 1780s. I contacted Scott Wilcox again and asked the date of the Farington album. The answer came back that it was variously dated 1790, *c.*1798 or 1810, all of which of course post-date the 1789 edition. This naturally puzzled me.

The more I studied the watercolours and the engravings, the more certain I was that these dates were wrong. So I contacted Scott again and he told me that the watermark on the paper used in the album showed 1794, suggesting that the watercolours could not have been produced before this date. However, he followed this up by letting me know that although the pen-and-ink and wash drawings were drawn straight on to the paper, further investigation showed that the watercolours were, in fact, on separate sheets mounted on it.

So it now looked possible that the watercolours might predate the engravings after all, even though the ink and wash drawings could not. However, now a new suggestion came up, which was that Farington, in a diary entry in 1800, was referring to these watercolours when he wrote: 'I began to wash outlines in Gray's journal' and 'I went on with drawing for Gray's journal.' I felt sure he could not have meant the watercolours or washes in the Yale album, but was referring to the drawings in preparation for Thomas Horne's 1816 volume of engravings.

By now I was convinced that the watercolours pre-dated the engravings, but found myself faced with a new and somewhat unusual suggestion, that as the date of the watercolours was uncertain, it was possible they had been painted from the engravings rather than vice versa. My instinct rejected this. Why would an artist copy an engraving of his own work so accurately? I wondered whether, where the volumes of 1789 and 1816 referred to engravings from 'drawings by

Joseph Farington', the word drawings in fact included watercolours. This led me to *A Short History of Engraving* published in 1908, in which the author A.H. Hind writes that Turner 'nearly always supplied his engravers with drawings in water-colour, and it is wonderful how in monochrome so much of the delicate shades of tone which depends in the original largely on colour, is preserved.' Clearly a watercolour could be considered a drawing.

However, the question as to whether the watercolours were used by the engraver for the engravings was finally resolved when Scott sent me copies of several sheets of manuscript notes that were loose in the album. One was a list of views that Farington either had painted or proposed to paint for Gray's journal. Some of these entries were written in red and others in black ink. At the bottom Farington adds an explanation: 'descriptions in black are coloured, the original drawings from which the prints were made'. And these 'descriptions' make up all the engravings in the 1789 volume.

As I studied the watercolours and engravings more carefully, I noticed instances where the watercolours and engravings differed in small ways one from the other. For example the watercolour of the 'Windermere from above Rarig [Rayrigg]' has two men (one on horseback) and a dog on the path, whereas the engraving shows a figure on horseback and two cows. There is a sepia sketch of this same scene showing three horsemen. Also in the 'North Entrance to Keswick' there is a reflection of the house in the river in the engraving but not in the watercolour. Could the engraver have made these changes on the instructions of the publisher to make the picture more picturesque and so increase its sales potential? It seems clear that this sort of adjustment was part of the process of converting drawings to engravings. Another interesting detail is that in some of the watercolours the figures have been painted on separate pieces of paper and have been attached to the painting. Were these figures painted by Farington or by some other hand?

Clearly, it was expected that many of the purchasers of these engravings would be visitors to the lakes or those planning a visit. To help these visitors, maps of the main lakes were produced in the 1780s by Peter Crosthwaite of Keswick. Crosthwaite was a tourist guide and he also had a small museum full of strange objects to which he would attract visitors by striking a large drum. His maps, he wrote, were 'a series of accurate maps of the principal lakes of Cumberland, Westmorland and Lancashire containing West's "stations" for viewing the scenery, depths of the various lakes at different parts from actual measurements;

their latitude and longitude; the course of ancient roads; the quaint form of the houses of the gentry; and other curious information to be found in no other work'. These maps were invaluable to tourists and have been incorporated into this book together with maps of Thirlmere, Grasmere and Rydal Water from James Clarke's *A Survey of the Lakes* published in 1789.

There is an entry in Farington's diary on 16 September 1806: 'Daniell Crosswaite Jnr of Keswick called . . . He told me the Views of the Lakes sell at Keswick better than ever.' He purchased twenty-two sets that year. Then on 8 January 1807: 'Byrne called in the evening & we agreed to offer the work of the Lakes to Crossthwaite for 300 guineas.' So the rights in the 1789 *Views of the Lakes* were transferred from Byrne and Farington to Crosthwaite.

Both volumes of engravings, those of 1789 and of 1816, include warnings that 'although these engravings are offered to the public as faithful representations of nature', visitors may already find changes where trees have grown, houses been built, or bridges collapsed due to flooding. And we find Wordsworth in his *Guide to the Lakes* complaining 'that the view of the Pleasure House from the Station [West's viewpoint on the west shore of Lake Windermere] near the Ferry has suffered much from larch plantations, this mischief, however, is gradually disappearing, and the larches under the management of the proprietor, Mr Curwen, are giving way to native wood.' Windermere, of course, suffered most from the Victorian enthusiasm for planting non-native species of evergreen trees and shrubs, and these, with their long lives, still obscure some key views.

It is, however, extraordinary how many of the Farington views can still be photographed after more than two hundred years. All the bridges (except that over the Derwent to the west of Keswick, which has never been replaced) have, at one time or another, been rebuilt, but those that exist today are nearly always in the same position and more often than not in a similar style. And only occasionally have new buildings blocked a view. The main problem in photographing Farington's views today has been, as Gilpin anticipated, the growth of trees. This has meant that on occasions my photographs could not be taken from Farington's viewpoints but instead from the closest points from which his views can still be seen.

*

Having decided on my planned layout for the watercolours, engravings and photographs, I gave thought to the words to go with them. I decided to reprint the text by William Cookson that appears opposite each engraving in the 1789 volume. This goes well with the watercolours, has an immediacy and freshness, and sometimes specifies the viewpoints taken by Farington. However, where I have inserted an engraving from the 1816 volume I have included with it a suitable passage from Thomas Horne, who himself toured the lakes when preparing his text (I have clearly marked each such passage 'TH'). Farington's diary entry of 27 March 1816 explains: 'Horne told me . . . [that his intention was] to give some account of the roads and inns and such circumstances as may amuse or be useful to the traveller who may visit that country to see its beauties.' Farington lent him three guidebooks for his tour, one of whch was West's *Guide*. It is clear from reading Horne's text that he was liberal in drawing on West.

PART FOUR

The Visual Tour

This section is based on Joseph Farington's watercolours and sepia sketches from the Farington album in the Yale Center for British Art. Most of the engravings and text come from *Views of the Lakes etc. in Cumberland and Westmorland: Engraved from drawings made by Joseph Farington R.A.* (with text by William Cookson). William Byrne, 1789.

The few additional engravings come from Thomas Hartwell Horne's *The Lakes of Lancashire, Westmorland and Cumberland: Delineated in forty-three engravings from the drawings of Joseph Farington R.A.* T. Cadell & W. Davies, 1816. The text taken from this volume is marked 'TH'. The maps of the individual lakes are taken from Peter Crosthwaite's *Maps of the Lake Disrict* (1794) with the exception of Thirlmere, Grasmere and Rydal Water, which come from James Clarke's *A Survey of the Lakes etc.*, 1789. The orientation of each map is made clear in its top left-hand corner.

The photographs are by John R Murray and were taken in 2009 and 2010.

The contemporary spelling of place names has been retained in the quoted extracts. Otherwise modern spelling has been used.

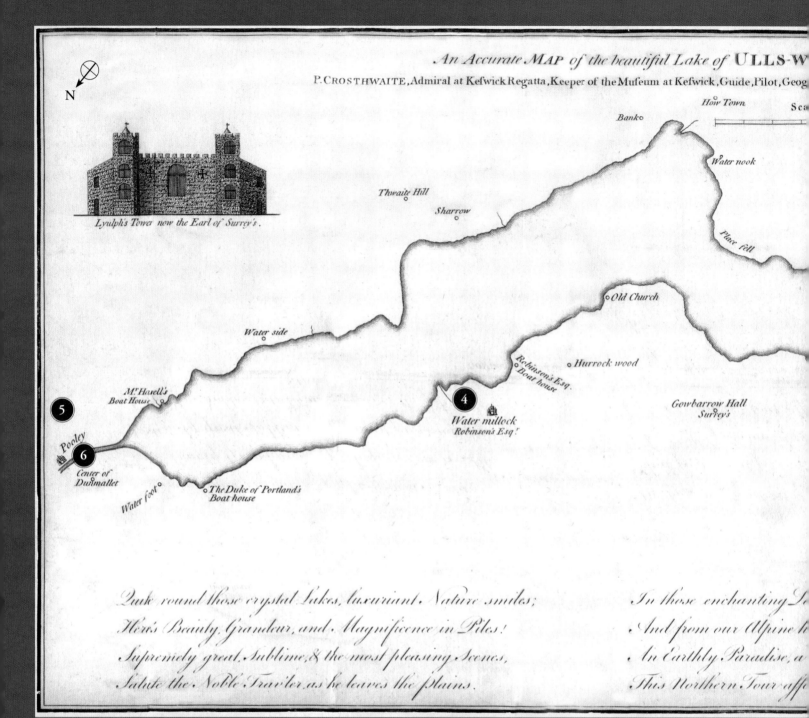

An Accurate MAP of the beautiful Lake of ULLS-W

P. CROSTHWAITE, Admiral at Keswick Regatta, Keeper of the Museum at Keswick, Guide, Pilot, Geog

Lyulph's Tower now the Earl of Surrey's.

Quit round those crystal Lakes, luxuriant Nature smiles;
Here's Beauty, Grandeur, and Magnificence in Piles!
Supremely great Sublime, & the most pleasing Scenes,
Salute the Noble Traveler as he leaves the Plains.

In those enchanting S
And from our Alpine h
An Earthly Paradise, a
This Northern Tour aff

Ullswater

1 View from the upper end of Ullswater
2 Across the lake to Patterdale
3 The 'Palace of Patterdale'
4 Watermillock looking south
5 The lower reach of Ullswater
6 Ullswater from Pooley Bridge

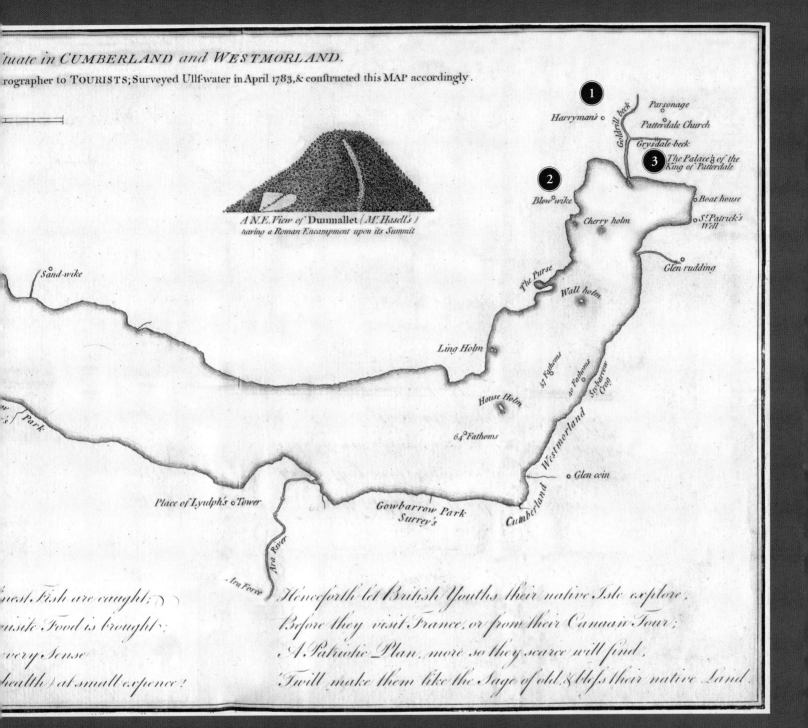

ituate in CUMBERLAND *and* WESTMORLAND.

rographer to TOURISTS; Surveyed Ullf-water in April 1783, & conftructed this MAP accordingly.

① Harryman's
Goldrill beck
Parsonage
Patterdale Church
Grysdale-beck
③ The Palace ⅋ of the King of Patterdale
② Blow wike
Boat house
Cherry holm
St Patrick's Well
Sand-wike
The Purse
Wall holm
Glen rudding
Ling Holm
51 Fathoms
40 Fathoms
St barrow Crag
House Holm
Westmorland
64 Fathoms
Glen coin
's Park
Place of Lyulph's ⊙ Tower
Gowbarrow Park
Surrey's
Cumberland
Ara River
Ara Force

A N.E. View of Dunmallet *(M.r Hasell's)*
having a Roman Encampment upon its Summit

neft Fish are caught;

uisite Food is brought;

very Sense

health) at small expence!

Henceforth let British Youths their native Isle explore,

Before they visit France, or from their Canaan Tour;

A Patriotic Plan, more so they scarce will find,

'Twill make them like the Sage of old & blefs their native Land.

1 | View from the upper end of Ullswater

'Ullswater lies to the east of Derwentwater and to the north of Winandermere [Windermere]. It is in size one of the most considerable of the lakes, being in length about eight miles, though its greatest breadth does not exceed one. Its direction like that of all the others is north and south. In point of beauty it is by many thought not inferior to any of them. In one respect it certainly has the superiority, viz. in affording the greatest variety.

This advantage it derives from its shape, which nearly resembles that of the letter Z, but without its angular sharpness. It is of course separated into three different reaches, winding at every turn round some bold projection of the surrounding mountains. This plate presents a prospect of the upper division looking down the lake, as viewed from the skirts of Martindale-Fell. The rivulet which serpentizes through the meadows is called Goldrill-beck, and is one of the principal feeders of the lake; it descends from Kirkston-fell, which forms the barrier between Windermere and Ullswater. This is the only division of the lake which is adorned with islands.'

watercolour (opposite) and engraving: *From the upper end of Ullswater looking north down the lake.*

photograph (right below): *This view, from the slopes of Martindale Fell, is probably a little lower than Farington's viewpoint.*

ENGRAVED BY W. BYRNE & T. MEDLAND, 1787

2 | Across the lake to Patterdale

'The view here represented is taken from the edge of Martindale-Fell looking over the bay of the lake, directly into Patterdale, where the chapel and palace are conspicuous. The mountains seen in the distance belong to the same chain with Helvellyn. These hills having their summits sharp and pointed resemble more the Alpine forms than any which are to be met with in this country. It is worthy of remark that in any one range or system of mountains a great similarity of outline generally prevails; the same strata perhaps, by whatever cause the inequalities of the earth's surface might have been produced, naturally disposing themselves into the same or similar forms.'

watercolour (opposite):
*Patterdale from Martindale
Fell looking west across the lake
with the Helvellyn range in the
background. There is a sepia
sketch of this view in the album
but without the figures (see page
137).*

engraving (right): *The boat
and sail that appear in this
engraving are not in the
watercolour.*

ENGRAVED BY W. BYRNE & T. MEDLAND, 1788

photograph (right): *Farington's
viewpoint was very difficult to
establish. However, the nearest
hill on the right across the water
can be clearly recognised in the
watercolour and engraving. The
trees on the far bank obscure a
view of Patterdale village.*

3 | The 'Palace of Patterdale'

'The village of Patterdale is situated near the head of Ullswater. It lies in a cove of mountains open in front to the southern reach of the lake. The building that forms the principal object in this view we have called the Palace of Patterdale, leaving the nature of its claim to that appellation to be explained by the following passage in Mr Gilpin's Observations on the Mountains and Lakes of Cumberland and Westmorland. "Among the cottages of this village, there is a house, belonging to a person of somewhat better condition; whose little estate, which he occupies himself, lies in the neighbourhood. As his property, inconsiderable as it is, is better than that of any of his neighbours, it has gained him the title of King of Patterdale, in which his family name is lost. His ancestors have long enjoyed the title before him. We had the honour of seeing this prince, as he took the diversion of fishing on the lake; and I could not help thinking, that if I were inclined to envy the situation of any potentate of Europe, it would be that of the King of Patterdale. The pride of Windsor or Versailles would shrink in a comparison with the magnificence of his Dominions."'

watercolour (opposite):
*Looking south-west to the
'Palace'. The scotch fir standing
at the time the drawing of
this subject was made had
attained 72 feet in height, and
was considered as a kind of
landmark to the vale.*

ENGRAVED BY W. BYRNE & J. LANDSEER, 1788, FIGURES BY J. HEATH

photograph (right):
*The original 'Palace of
Patterdale' no longer exists but a
more recent building can be seen
through the trees in the centre.*

ENGRAVED BY J. SCOTT 1815

4 | Watermillock looking south

'Water-Millock, the celebrated seat of the late Mr Robinson, a truly enviable residence is seen in the first distance near the centre of the accompanying view, deeply sequestered amid beech and sycamore trees which shelter it from every inclement blast. Beneath is the lower end of the first reach of Ullswater which here takes a majestic sweep. Opposite is Swarth Fell, a naked rock, deeply scarred by successive storms and torrents. The mountains which form the back-screen, along the right side of the lake, are the craggy steeps of Helvellyn and other rugged eminences of inferior elevation.

engraving (above): *View from Watermillock and the Lower end of Ullswater. (There is no Farington watercolour of this view in the Yale album, nor an engraving in the 1789 volume.)*

photograph (above): *This photograph was taken close to the viewpoint of the engraving but in the engraving the mountains have been stylised. There were only a few trees when Farington drew this view.*

On the left of the lake is Martindale Bay, necessarily given but imperfectly in our engraving, on whose shores, we were told, echoes of singular grandeur may be obtained by firing a cannon. The sound of the explosion is repeated like peals of thunder, of various duration, sometimes reverberating in hollow murmers, and sometimes seeming like the crash of mountains: the report of every discharge is said to be seven times distinctly re-echoed.' TH

5 | The lower reach of Ullswater

'This plate gives a view of the lowest reach of Ullswater. It is of a very different character from the other two divisions. Those appear to the eye completely environed by impending mountains, whereas this, if Dunmallet were removed, would lie entirely open to the adjacent country. Dunmallet is a hill of a regular conic form, of no great height, and somewhat formally planted with wood. On its top are the vestiges of a Roman fortress, well adapted, like that on Castle-crag, at the head of Derwentwater, to command all the avenues of the country. The view is taken near the farmhouse called Bowerbank overlooking the village of Pooley which stands on the outlet of the lake.

The river here takes the name of Emont and after a course of eight or ten miles falls into the Eden. The wood rising on the right of the foreground is part of Dunmallet. In the first distance near the centre appears Watermellock, the habitation of Mr Robinson, charmingly situated upon an eminence. The hills on the left are Place-fell, etc. In the most remote distance rises Helvellyn which disputes pre-eminence in respect of altitude with Skiddaw and Cross-fell.'

watercolour (opposite): *The lower reach of Ullswater from Bowerbank Farm above Pooley (see the sepia sketch on page 138).*

engraving (right): *Unlike the watercolour, this engraving includes, on the right towards the bottom of the field, three horses, a woman and a child.*

ENGRAVED BY W. BYRNE & T. MEDLAND, 1787

photograph (right): *The viewpoint of the watercolour is carefully specified as 'taken near the farmhouse called Bowerbank' which is above the village of Pooley. This photograph was taken close to this position but the expansion of the village and the growth of trees have obscured the lake, although it can just be glimpsed in the distance above the houses through the trees.*

6 | Ullswater from Pooley Bridge

'Two miles further bring us to the little village of Pooley, pleasantly situated at the foot of Ulswater, and having, besides the embellishments of wood and water, a great accession of beauty from Dunmallard Hill, so called from the great resort of wild fowl thither from the lake. With this hill the village is connected by a neat bridge over the Emond, whence the annexed view of Ulswater has been taken. In the foreground on the left appears part of the village of Pooley, already mentioned, where there is a commodious little inn, much frequented by anglers as well as visitors of the lake itself: boats may here be obtained for navigating Ulswater, with guides, and cannon and ammunition for awakening the loud echoes from the surrounding hills. The mountain immediately behind the village is called Barton Park, beyond which arised Martindale Fell; and further on, the craggy rock of Hallin Hag. At the foot of these flows the first reach of the lake.' TH

sepia sketch (opposite): *The lower reach of Ullswater from Pooley Bridge (called Barton Bridge by Thomas Gray). This sepia sketch differs in many respects from the 1816 volume engraving (the boat in the foreground is absent in the sketch, and the rocks in the left foreground do not appear in the engraving). This sketch was clearly not used by the engraver.*

ENGRAVED BY S. MIDDIMAN, 1815

photograph (right): *This photograph was taken from the bridge. The houses in the trees that appear in the sepia sketch and the engraving no longer exist.*

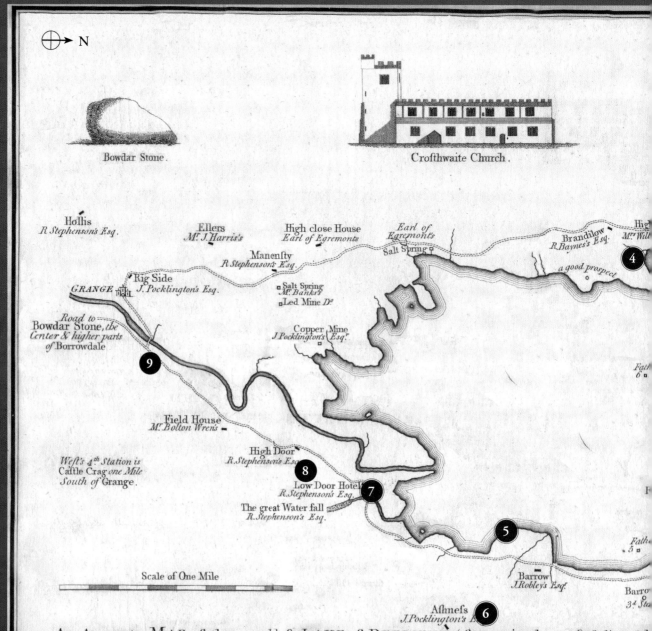

Bowdar Stone.

Crofthwaite Church.

An Accurate MAP of the matchlefs LAKE of DERWENT, (fituate in the moft delightful
pointed out, beginning near Keswick, and numbering to the Left. Pocklington's Island is the property of J. Pocklington Esq.ʳ Lord
View of Crofthwaite Church, and a North View of Skiddow in the Twilight; taken from the Beautiful Field (Sir Michael le Fleming's,
Author's own Invention (and not by Guess) who makes Skiddow 1050 Yards above the Level of Derwent. The Church 47 Yards long; a
Surveyed &c. by P. CROSTHWAITE Admiral at Keswick Regatta; who keeps the Museum at Keswick, &c

Derwentwater

1 View over Keswick to Skiddaw
2 North entrance to Keswick
3 Derwentwater looking south
4 View to Skiddaw down Derwentwater

5 Looking south to Lodore Falls
6 View over Derwentwater to Bassenthwaite Lake
7 Lodore Falls
8 Derwentwater and Skiddaw from Lodore
9 Looking towards Grange in Borrowdale

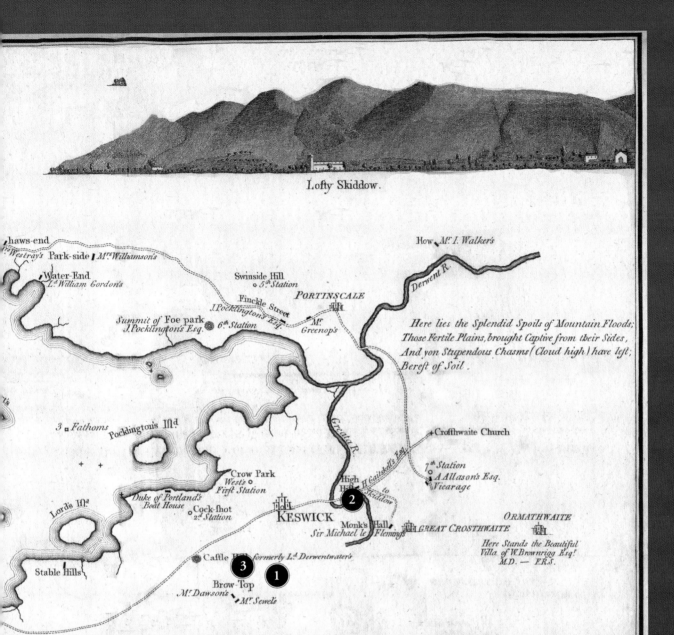

Lofty Skiddow.

haws-end
Westray's Park-side   Mr. Williamson's   How ⟶ Mr. I. Walker's

Water-End
L.d William Gordon's

Swinside Hill
5.th Station

Finckle Street
J. Pocklington's Esq.   PORTINSCALE

Summit of Foe park
J. Pocklington's Esq.   6.th Station

Mr.
Greenop's

Derwent R.

Here lies the Splendid Spoils of Mountain Floods;
Those Fertile Plains, brought Captive from their Sides,
And yon Stupendous Chasms (Cloud high) have left;
Bereft of Soil.

3 ⟶ Fathoms   Pocklington's Ind.

Crofthwaite Church

Greata R.

Crow Park
West's
First Station

Duke of Portland's
Boat House

Cock-fhot
2.d Station

Lord's Ind.

Stable Hills

Castle Hill formerly L.d Derwentwater's

Brow-Top
Mr. Dawson's   Mr. Sewel's

High
High   H. Gaitskell's Esq.   to
Skiddow

7.th Station
A. Allason's Esq.
Vicarage

KESWICK

Monk's Hall
Sir Michael le Flemings   GREAT CROSTHWAITE

ORMATHWAITE

Here Stands the Beautiful
Villa of W. Brownrigg Esq.r
M.D. — F.R.S.

2   **3**   **1**

perhaps ever Human Eye beheld) near *KESWICK, CUMBERLAND;* with West's seven Stations
erly L.d Derwentwater's; Rampsholm Ifland, d.º d.º St. Herbert's Ifland, Sir Gilfred Lawson's. Above is a S.W. View of Bowdar Stone; a North
d Stone, are taken from one Scale; being ⅟₂₀ of an Inch to one Yard; and Skiddow ⅟₂₀ of an Inch to 100 Yards; by a Quadrant of the
Pinnacle, 20 Yards; Bowdar Stone 21 Yards long, and 11 high.
Geographer & Hydrographer to the Nobility and Gentry, who make the Tour of the Lakes.

ENGRAVED BY W. BYRNE, 1815

1 | View over Keswick to Skiddaw

'From its central position, Keswick may be considered as the metropolis of the Lakes; it is much frequented by strangers making the tour of the Lakes. Post-chaises go from Keswick to Penrith, every Monday, Wednesday and Friday, and return on intermediate days. Similar conveyances also pass through this town, from Kendal and Ambleside to Cockermouth and Whitehaven . . . The weekly market, which is held on Saturdays, is abundantly supplied, and is particularly celebrated for its delecate mountain-mutton, and for the variety of exquisitely nice fresh-water fish obtained from the neighbouring lakes. The manufactures now chiefly carried on at Keswick are coarse woollen goods, blankets, kerseys etc. Here are two museums, one or both of which should be visited by every tourist . . . The proprietors of both of these museums are intelligent guides: and both of them contain specimens of almost every variety of the mineral substances found in Cumberland together with numerous kinds of plants, British and Roman antiquities, coins, and other rarities both British and foreign.' TH

engraving (above): *'Towering Skiddaw, wrapt in awful shade, / Monarch of mountains, rears his mighty head; / Darkening with frowns fair Keswick's beauteous vale, / He views beneath the gathering tempest sail'* (Thomas Hartwell Horne's Lakes of Lancashire etc.).

photograph (above): *It is surprising that this field has survived the expansion of Keswick and that the view can be photographed today. Houses have been built all around it. This photograph has been taken from Fenton, close to Castlerigg Manor off Manor Brow.*

2 | North entrance to Keswick

'Keswick stands on the north of Derwentwater, and at no great distance from it. It is a small market town chiefly deriving its importance from its situation, being usually made the headquarters of the inquisitive traveller. The point of view is at the entrance of the road from Cockermouth. The bridge in the foreground is over the Greata, which joins the Derwent a little below in its course from Derwent- to Bassenthwaite-water. Behind the houses on the right stands Castlett-crag at the foot of which runs the road to Lodore. The rocks which serve as a background to the scene are Wallow-crag, Eve-crag, etc. hanging over the eastern side of the lake. Keswick is eighteen miles distant from Windermere, and fourteen from Ullswater. It ought to be observed here, as it was done before with respect to the timber and coppice-woods, that the bridges in this country are liable to perpetual alterations on account of the violence of the torrents [the floods and loss of bridges in 2009 were nothing new]; it is not therefore to be wondered if the representation given of them should sometimes vary from the present form.'

watercolour (opposite): *North entrance to Keswick and the bridge over the river Greta with Castle Crag in the background. There is also a sepia sketch of this view in the Yale album that shows what appear to be washer-women on the near bank of the river, only one man and a dog walking towards the bridge and no figures on the bridge itself (see page 136).*

ENGRAVED BY W. BYRNE & T. MEDLAND, 1787

photograph (right):
This bridge is a more recent replacement, although it is in the same position as the original. However, the Greta River seen in this photograph runs tight up beside the road, although in Farington's painting and the engraving it is sweeping round, leaving a bank between the road and the water. At first it seemed that the river's course had been realigned at some point but James Clarke's A Survey of the Lakes etc. of 1789 (not totally reliable), with its detailed maps and plans, suggests that the Greta ran tight beside the road in Gray's day and if so Farington's foreground is artist's licence.

3 | Derwentwater looking south

'Half a mile further brought us to Borough Top (pronounced Brow Top), another eminence about half a mile on this side [south-east] of Keswick. Here, the view, delineated in the annexed engraving, burst upon the eye with inconceivable splendour, and exhibits the general form of Derwentwater much better, perhaps, than from any other point of view. The craggy mountain which first presents itself on the left is known by the name of Wallow Crag: the hollow in its crumbling summit is called Lady's Rake, from the generally received tradition, that by this steep, the ambitious Lady Derwentwater effected her escape when the Earl was arrested for High Treason. The low mountains in front are Grange Fells, in which Castle-Crag is conspicuous, and behind these, Bull-Crag, Sergeant's Crag and Eagle-Crag (once celebrated for being the resort of those birds of prey), successively rear their heads, forming a conspicuous part of Borrodale Fells; and the amphitheatre of mountains is closed by Causeway Pike and Grisedale Pike, which is two thousand seven hundred and fifty-six feet above sea level. At the foot of these stupendous heights appears the Lake itself, which is broken into several pretty bays.' TH

ENGRAVED BY F. R. HAY, 1816

photograph (right): *This photograph was taken from between two houses in the built-up area of Manor Brow just below Brough Top. A photograph could not be taken from Brough Top itself as a plantation of trees obscures the view.*

4 | View of Skiddaw down Derwentwater

'This plate exhibits a view of the mountain of Skiddaw, and the Lake of Derwentwater, as seen from Brandelow-Woods on its western shore. The town of Keswick appears on the opposite side, a little to the right. Skiddaw may be ranked amongst the highest hills in the island: Its greatest elevation is 3270 feet above the level of the sea, and not much less above that of the lake. The surface of the mounstain is smooth and verdant. It may not be improper here to observe, that the hills amongst which these lakes are situated, assume a very different character, according to the nature of the rock they are composed of; this is either rag [a local word for course stone] or limestone. Where the former prevails the mountain has a foreboding and somewhat savage aspect; its surface is deformed with swampy patches, or pits of Turbury, and the pasturage for the most part is mossy, heathy and wet. Those temporary cataracts, which in rainy weather perpetually attract the notice of the stranger, are peculiar to this species of mountains. Those which consist of limestone, though generally of inferior height, present an appearance more chearful and aggreable to the eye.'

watercolour (opposite): *Derwentwater and Skiddaw looking north from Brandelhow Wood. The cows and figures in the foreground are painted on a separate piece of paper attached to the painting.*

photograph (right): *It was not easy to discover Farington's exact viewpoint but this position on the north edge of Brandelhow Wood seems about right. The peninsula across the water is now planted with evergreens that distort its original shape.*

5 | Looking south to Lodore Falls

'Lowdore Waterfall is generally claimed one of the most striking objects of the kind in this country; its accompaniments are uncommonly picturesque and grand. These indeed compose of themslves a scene which cannot but interest the spectator, even when the fall of the water, which depends upon the state of the weather, is inconsiderable. The stupendous craggs between which the torrent precipitates itself broken into the boldest forms, are shagged with trees hanging everywhere in the most fantastic shapes, from the fissures of the rock. The height of the Fall itself Mr Gray conjectures to be about two hundred feet. At some distance above the Fall the stream proceeds from a lake about a mile in circumference. To this sequestered spot travellers are seldom conducted, though they might perhaps think themselves amply recompensed for their trouble, by a sight of lake and village near it called Wawtenleth [*sic*]. The point from whence this view is taken is a little to the right of the road leading from Keswick into Borrowdale, near the side of Derwentwater, where it forms a small bay.'

watercolour (opposite): *View of Lodore Falls from the east shore of the lake a quarter of a mile north of the falls. The cows and figures on the left are painted on a separate piece of paper attached to the painting (see the different version of the Falls on pages 138–9).*

Many painters of the time depicted Lodore Falls as a kind of Niagara of the Lakes but it is unlikely that these falls ever burst forth in this way. William Gilpin wrote in 1776: 'Lodoor was a great penury, when we past it. Instead of roaring over the mighty rocks which form its descent, it fell gently down gliding among them with feeble tone.'

ENGRAVED BY W. BYRNE & T. MEDLAND, 1785

photograph (right): *The falls cannot be seen from this viewpoint today, but they can just be seen from the lakeside road beside the Lodore Hotel when there is a good flow of water and no leaves on the trees.*

6 | View over Derwentwater to Bassenthwaite Lake

'This view is intended to convey a general idea of the Valley of Keswick. Ashness, from where it is taken, is on the summit of the rocks which hang ovr the road leading to Lowdore, distant from Keswick about two miles and a half. No other point can perhaps be fixed upon where the several features which distinguish the romantic vale will appear to be so strongly marked. The elevation is sufficient to command an extensive prospect, without so far reducing its component parts as materially to affect their importance. A great part of Derwentwater, including its four principal islands, is in front, and the Lake of Bassenthwaite in the distance. The stream which forms the communication between them is only to be traced by the flatness and luxuriance of the adjacent meadows. The foot of Bassenthwaite is distant about ten miles from Ashness. From the margin of this lake on the right rises Skiddaw, on whose skirts appear a part of the town of Keswick; the rest is concealed from the view of Cockbut-hill. On the left of Derwentwater are Newlands and Thornthwaite fells. Beyond there are the woods of Wythop hanging over the more distant lake. The whole view is terminated by Caer-Mot, a hill remarkable for still retaining the evident traces of a Roman encampment.'

watercolour (opposite):
*Derwentwater and the Vale of
Keswick from Ashness looking
north: Bassenthwaite Lake is
in the distance. The figures in
the foreground are painted on a
separate piece of paper attached
to the painting. There is also a
sepia sketch of this view in the
Yale album but instead of two
men leading a horse carrying
hay there is a single man on a
horse (see page 137).*

ENGRAVED BY W. BYRNE & T. MEDLAND, 1787

photograph (right): *Farington's
viewpoint was from Ashness
bridge. Becouse of the planting
of trees the view was only
possible from about 75 yards
further up the side of the fell.*

7 | Lodore Falls

'In dry weather the fall is inconsiderable, and its grandeur is consequently much diminished; but when charged with the thousand streams which a storm pours occasionally from the mountains, the bubbling cascade becomes a stupendous cataract, which, rushing down an enormous pile of protruding crags, rolls along in uninterrupted volume and impetuous velocity. The scene at such a time is magnificent. The tremendous roar of the rushing water, which on serene evenings (we are assured) can be distincly heard at a distance of ten or twelve miles, is perfectly in unison with its rocky accompaniment. The view, now under consideration, was made when the whole scene lay open to the eye and the torrents of rain had filled every cavity of the fall, and flooded the brook proceeding from it. The river Lowdore, which is one of chief feaders of the lake, takes it rise in the valley of Watenlath. . . . [The rock to the left of our view] is Gowder Crag commanding from its summit a most extensive view over the lakes of Derwentwater and Bassenthwaite . . . The lower mountain to the right of the cataract is Shepherd's Crag. The best station for seeing [the falls] to advantage is through an opening in the grove directly above the hut, which appears on the left of our view, and was formerly a mill.' TH

sepia sketch (opposite):
*This sepia wash differs in
a number of ways from the
engraving and would not have
been used by the engraver. In the
engraving a girl appears with a
water pitcher on her head and
the horse is being followed, not
led. The falls would never have
appeared like this.*

ENGRAVED BY T. LANDSEER FSA, 1816

photograph (right): *You can
only see the waterfall through
the trees before the leaves come
out and when a lot of water is
cascading down. There is still a
small building on the left of the
bridge. This picture was taken
from underneath the modern
bridge.*

ENGRAVED BY J. SCOTT, 1815

8 | Derwentwater and Skiddaw from Lodore

'On turning from viewing the Cataract of Lowdore, we had before us the charming view of Derwentwater, with Skiddaw for its backgrownd, which is delineated in the engraving. Below are the meadows of Lowdore, on which some groupes of cattle were grazing: beyond these, in the transparent lake, were the three wooded islands, St Herbert's, Rampsholm, and Lord's Island. On the distand shore appears Crossthwaite or Keswick church; and behind this Skiddaw reared his majestic head, on which we could distinctly see numerous patches of snow.' TH

engraving (above): *There was no original sketch of this scene in the Yale album, although an engraving after Farington appears in the 1816 volume. I have included this as it is interesting to see how accurately Skiddaw in the distance has been depicted in the engraving.*

photograph (above): *I had to climb up into the woods beside the Lodore Hotel to find this viewpoint. It appears that the lake came up much closer to Lodore Falls in Farington's day.*

9 | Looking towards Grange in Borrowdale

'Grange in Borrowdale consists of a few houses standing on the west side of the river Derwent, about a mile above its entrance into the lake. This village is a mile distant from the waterfall of Lowdore, and about five from Keswick. In this spot is formed by the impending mountains what Mr Gray calls "The Gorge of Borrowdale". Concealed from the sight by the precipice on the foregrownd stands Castle-Crag, nearly of the same form with the wooded rock in front, but of much larger dimensions. On its top are the vestiges of a Roman fort, the garrison of which might receive intimation by signal from the station on Caer-Mot of any hostile attempts from the Northern quarter. The dale, secluding itself beyond this hill, continues to exhibit for a few miles the wildest and most romantic scenes, forming a striking contrast to the open display of magnificence which characterises the Vale of Keswick. Except in the dry season, the Derwent affords a passage to boats from the Lake up to the bridge; the extreme transparency of the water never escapes the observation of the traveller.'

watercolour (opposite):
Grange in Borrowdale and the
bridge over the river Derwent.
There is also a sepia version of
this view in the Yale album and
a variation of it in the 1816
volume (see page 140).

ENGRAVED BY W. BYRNE & T. MEDLAND, 1784

photograph (right): *The bridge*
is more recent but its position is
the same as in the original and
the road follows the old route.
The roofs of Grange can just
be seen through the trees at the
right end of the bridge.

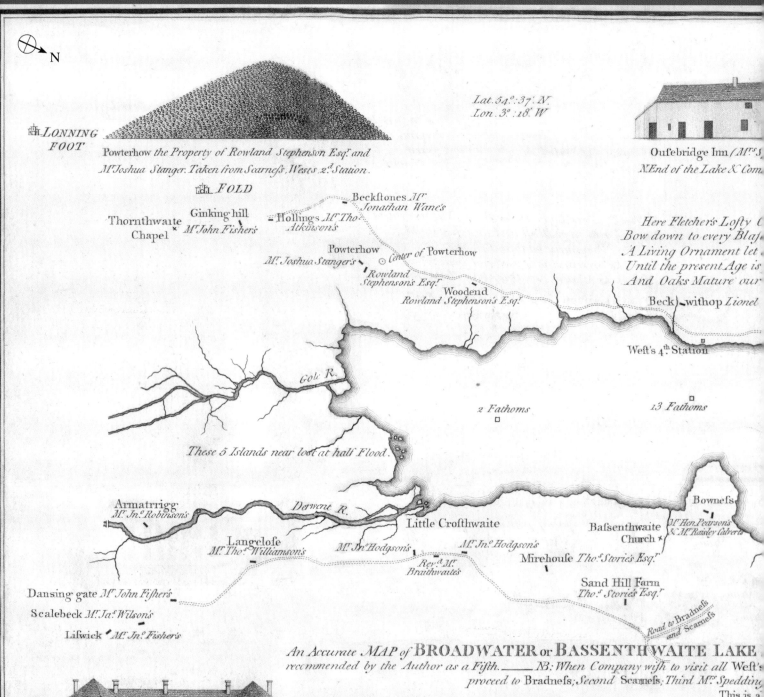

Bassenthwaite Lake

① Bassenthwaite Lake from the North

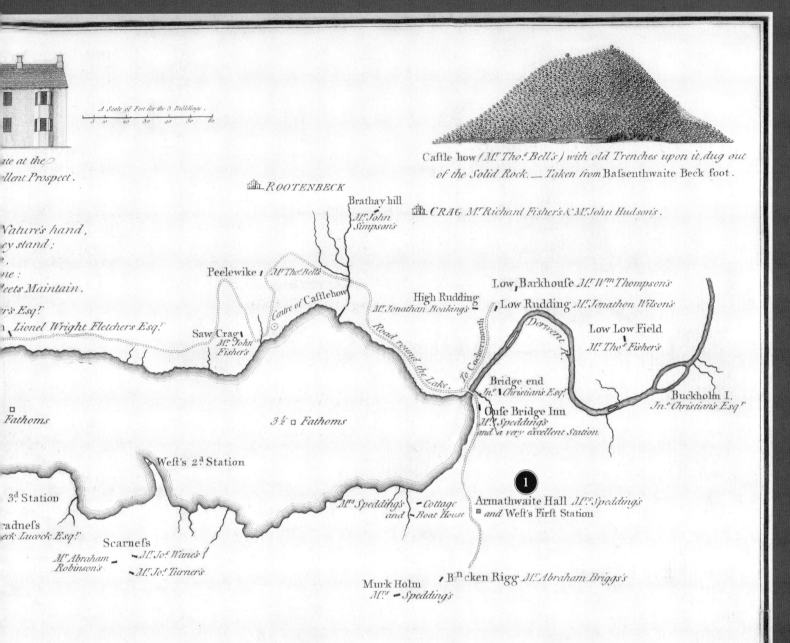

A Scale of Feet for the 3 Buildings.
5 10   20   30   40   50   60

...te at the...
...llent Prospect .

...Nature's hand ,
...ey stand ;
...e :
...eets Maintain .
...r's Esq.?

...Lionel Wright Fletchers Esq.?

☖ ROOTENBECK

Brathay hill
Mr John
Simpson's

Castle how (Mr Thos Bell's) with old Trenches upon it, dug out
of the Solid Rock. — Taken from Bassenthwaite Beck foot .

☖ CRAG Mr Richard Fisher's & Mr John Hudson's .

Peelewike ∎ Mr Tho.s Bell's

Centre of Castlehow

Saw Crag ∎
Mr John
Fisher's

High Rudding
Mr Jonathan Boaking's

Low Barkhouse Mr Wm Thompson's
Low Rudding Mr Jonathon Wilson's

Derwent R.

Low Low Field
Mr Thos Fisher's

Road round the Lake.

To Cockermouth

Bridge end
Jn.o Christian's Esq.r

Buckholm I.
Jn.o Christian's Esq.r

∎ Fathoms   3½ ▢ Fathoms

West's 2.d Station

Ouse Bridge Inn
Mrs Spedding's
and a very excellent Station

3.d Station

...radnefs
...ck Lucock Esq.r

Scarnefs

Mr Abraham
Robinson's

Mr Jos Wane's

Mr Jos Turner's

Mrs Spedding's
and

Cottage
Boat House

① Armathwaite Hall Mrs Spedding's
∎ and West's First Station

Murk Holm
Mrs Spedding's

Bn cken Rigg Mr Abraham Briggs's

...ICK, CUMBERLAND with WEST's Four Stations pointed out thus ▢ & Ousebridge Inn
... go from KESWICK down the East Side of this Lake; it will be most convenient First to
...Inn, and from thence along the Western Shore to the last.
...tiful Lake .

The South the Vale of Keswick ever grand,
And winding Shoars with variegated Wood:
Compleat the Scene and Circumscribe the Flood.

...e .

...de, Pilot, Geographer & Hydrographer to the Nobility & Gentry, who make the Tour of the Lakes .

Armathwaite Hall Mrs Spedding's

VOLUME ENGRAVED BY F. R. HAY, 1815

1 | Bassenthwaite Lake from the north

'Bassenthwaite Lake or Broad Water, as it is sometimes called, is nearly four miles north of Derwentwater, having, in the east, the beautiful and extensive vale of Bassenthwaite, forming several pretty bays; behind which the mighty Skiddaw (on the left of the engraving) rears its lofty head. Opposite, on the west, is a range of humble mountains, called Wythop Brows, which fall abruptly to the water's edge, these declivities are partly rocky and partly covered with thick woods, consisting chiefly of young oaks, growing out of old stems. The mansion in the foreground is Armathwaite Hall, the seat of Sir Frederick Fletcher Vane, Bart, who has made very considerable plantations; so that the house, which in our view [in the engraving above] appears to be exposed, is now completely embowered in young and flourishing woods. The other mansion, on the left [in the distance], beneath Skiddaw, is Mire-House, the residence of John Spedding, Esq. who, since 1802, has also made extensive plantations in its neighbourhood, spreading over a considerable part of the adjoining mountain.' TH

engraving (above): *Looking south up Bassenthwaite Lake from above Armathwaite Hall. There is no watercolour or engraving of this scene in the 1789 volume.*

photograph (above): *Trees obscure the view from above Armathwaite Hall. The only view possible of this aspect of the lake was from a gap in the trees that stretch along the north shore.*

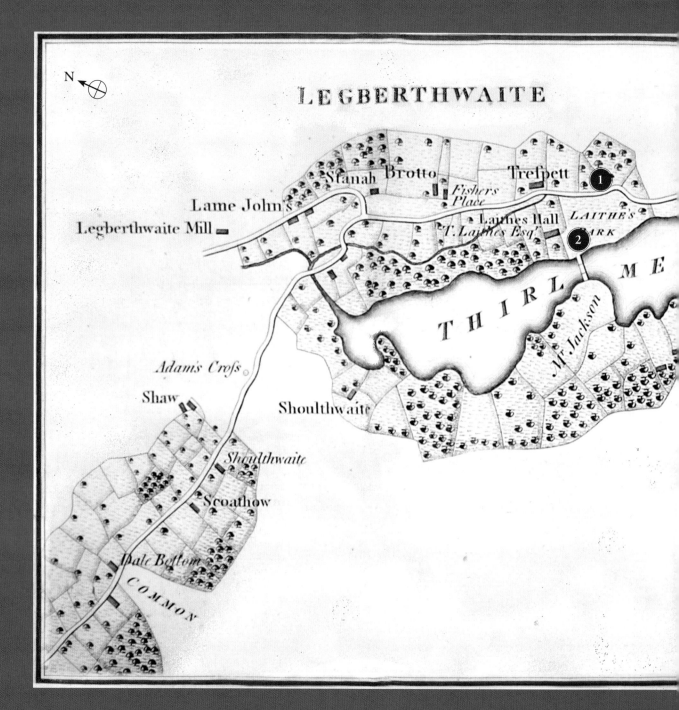

Thirlmere

1 View looking north from Six-mile-stone
2 Looking north-west down Thirlmere

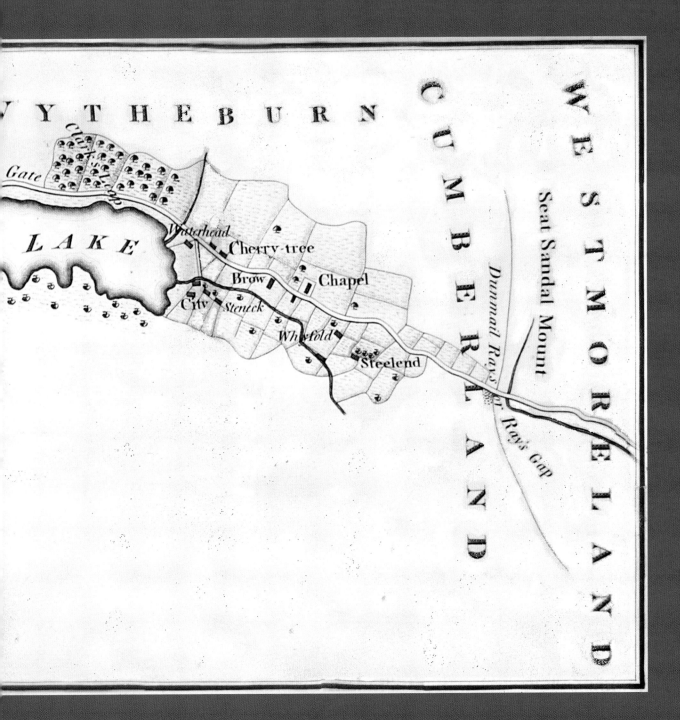

WYTHEBURN

CUMBERLAND

WESTMORELAND

Gate

LAKE

Watterhead

Cherry-tree

Brow

Chapel

City   Steneck

Whytfold

Steelend

Seat Sandal Mount

Dunmail Rays or Rays Gap

1 | View looking north from Six-mile-stone

'The road from Ambleside to Keswick affords a series of romantic and pictureque views . . . After passing the charming scenery of Rydal, and the wild environs which surround the lake of that name, from the top of a steep ascent, the peaceful embosomed Grasmere presents itself. Pursuing the way from this sequestered and beautiful retreat, by a long ascending road, a height is gained which commands the vale left behind, so as to produce what is termed a bird's-eye-view. Grasmere becomes a small feature in this extensive landscape, and the enclosures of the cultivated vale are crowded together like the divisions in a map. Descending on the north side, Wythburn or Leathes Water [Thirlmere], comes into view, which is of a wild and barren character. The road passes a considerable way on the margin of that lake, when it becomes again steep and winding; but the tediousness of Alpine travelling is compensated by the scene which opens from the six-mile stone, on this side of Keswick. Between lofty mountains on the right, and rocks of high and rude forms on the left, passes the narrow green vale of Legberthwaite, which is divided into small enclosures, and peopled with a few cots. The vale is terminated by the romantic Rock of St John; behind which rises Saddleback . . .'

watercolour (opposite):
View looking north from Six-mile-stone on the road from Ambleside to Keswick. The vale ends with the great Rock of St John, Saddleback is in the background and Farington depicts it very accurately. There is also a sepia sketch of this (see page 141).

ENGRAVED BY W. BYRNE & J. LANDSEER, 1789

photograph (right): *This photograph was taken at Six-mile-stone. As can be seen, the modern road runs down to the left following the route of the old road and the Rock of St John is prominent. Saddleback closes off the end of the valley.*

2 | Looking north-west down Thirlmere

'Thirlmere or Wyburn Lake, also called Leathes-Water, is a narrow irregular
sheet of water, indented with numerous little bays, about four miles in length,
skirting, on its eastern side, along the immense base of Helvellyn, and receiving
supplies from numerous torrents that precipitate themselves down the sides of
that huge mountain, as well as from the surrounding mountains, which cast
a deep brown shade over the surface of the water. . . . There is one peculiar
feature belonging to Thirlmere, which distinguishes it from all the other
lakes of Cumberland and Westmorland. About the middle, the land projects
upwards of three hundred feet, and contracts the water to the size of a small
river, rapid but not deep, over which has been thrown an Alpine bridge of
three arches, if such they may be called, which consist only of one or two stout
oaken planks with a hand-rail for the passenger's security. The approach to
this bridge is over a rude causeway of rough stones, upon which the arches are
fixed; and beyond these the lake instantly resumes its former breadth.' TH

sepia sketch (opposite):
Looking down Thirlmere showing the old 'celtic bridge'. This sketch was not used for the engraving. There is no engraving of this view in the 1789 volume.

ENGRAVED BY F. R. HAY, 1816

photograph (right): *At the end of the nineteenth century Thirlmere was turned into a reservoir to supply water to Manchester. This raised the level of the water by about 40 feet and submerged farms and homesteads as well as the old 'celtic bridge' shown in both the sketch and engraving. This photograph was taken from a position on the bank close to where the track once led down to the bridge. The great outcrop of rock on the left side of the lake in the sketch and engraving can be seen here but less distinctly as it is now well wooded. Thirlmere was treeless at the end of the eighteenth century.*

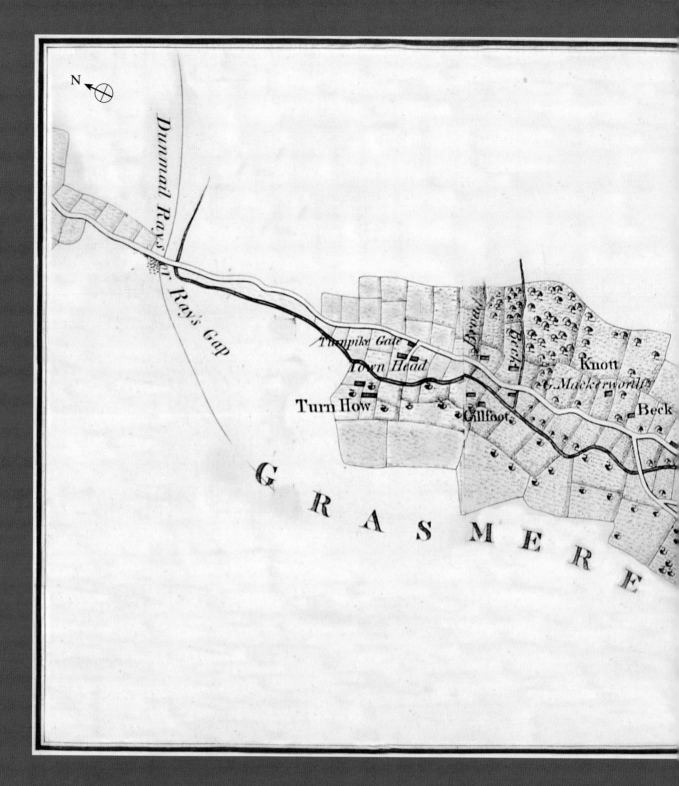

On the map: *Dunmail Rays or Rays Gap*, *Turnpike Gate*, *Town Head*, *Turn How*, *Gillfoot*, *Brook*, *Brook*, *Knott*, *G. Mackerworth*, *Beck*, **GRASMERE**

Grasmere and Rydal Water

① Looking north across Grasmere to Helm Crag

② Rydal Water

③ Lower waterfall, Rydal

④ Looking south towards Windermere

⑤ Rydal Bridge

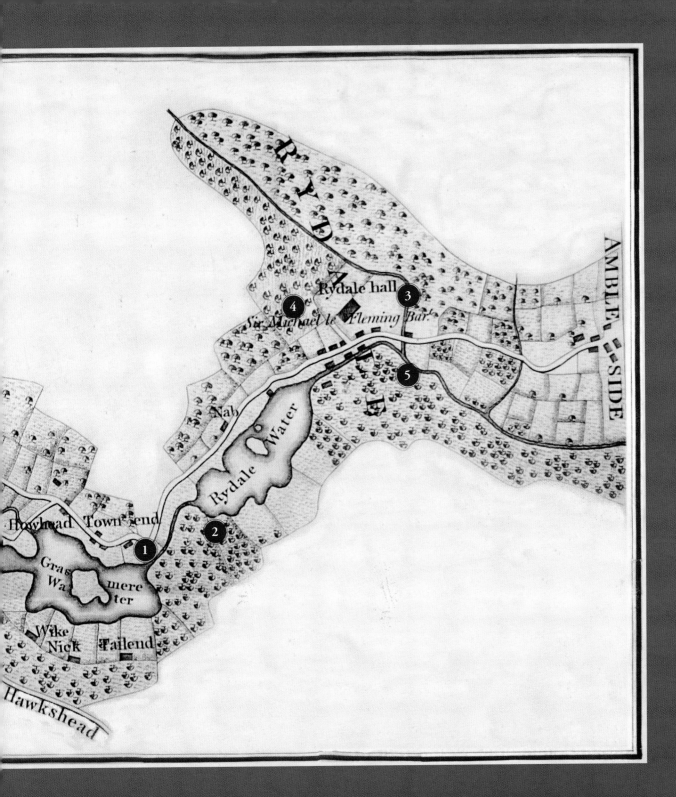

RYDAL

AMBLESIDE

Rydale hall

Sir Michael le Fleming Bar.^t

④

③

⑤

Nab

Rydale Water

Hawshead Town end

②

①

Gras mere Wa ter

Wike Nick Tailend

Hawkshead

1 | Looking across Grasmere to Helm Crag

'Grasmere lies about four miles from Ambleside, near the road to Keswick. The vale in which it is situated is about four miles in circumference. In the centre of this vale, beyond the lake, stands the church and village of Grasmere, above which rises Helme-Crag, of a pyramidal form, and particulary distinguished by the broken outline of its summit. On the right of this mountain are Steel-Fell and Seat-Sandle; between them passes the road leading to Keswick, the highest point of which, as seen in this view, marks the situation of Dunmail-Raise, a heap of stones, which perpetuate the name and fall of the last King of Cumberland, defeated there by the Saxon monarch, Edmund, about the year 945. Grasmere contains one island, and is not of great extent, but, with its vale, possesses particular beauty. Enriched with cultivation, the vale exhibits a variegated scene of peaceful industry, while the lofty mountains which surround it throw a gentle shade over the bosom of the secluded retreat, which adds to the air of stillness and retirement.'

watercolour (opposite):
Looking north across Grasmere to Grasmere village with Helm Crag in the background. The two men with the horse and cart in the foreground are painted on a separate piece of paper attached to the painting. There is also a sepia sketch of this view in the Yale album with three characters in the foreground instead of the horse and cart and two men and no figures behind them silhouetted against the lake (see page 141).

ENGRAVED BY B. T. POUNCY, 1785

photograph (right): *This photograph is taken from the south-east end of Grasmere. It is impossible to take it from Farington's exact viewpoint as this view is now completely obscured by trees.*

2 | Rydal Water

'Rydal-Mere [Rydal Water] is least in extent of any of the lakes in this set. It is about two miles from Ambleside, and is formed by the stream of Rothay, in its course from Grasmere to Winandermere [Windermere]. The view given here has the appearance of an amphitheatre. The wild and desert air of the mountains, which arise immediately from its margin, exhibit a striking contrast to the luxuriance and cultivation of the vale of Grasmere. The variety of character assumed by the several lakes affords no small source of entertainment to the admirer of picturesque beauty. The richness of the culivated vale, and the savage aspect of the rocks, with the infinite variety of combinations they admit of, present him with the beautiful and sublime through all their possible gradations. He will remark too with pleasure, that this country, so far from having suffered by the hand of art, derives considerable advantage from accidental circumstances. That the white or grey-stone cottages, with ash-coloured slating, are scattered over the face of the country, enlivening the landscape, without affecting its simplicity; and that even the dark hue of the fir tree, which is frequently planted near them, is beautifully contrasted with the brilliancy of the silver rock.'

watercolour (opposite): *View south across Rydal Water. The figures and sheep are painted on a separate piece of paper attached to the painting. There is a sepia sketch of this view but with horsemen instead of sheep and there is an engraving of this variant in the 1816 volume but with two figures instead of the horsemen (see page 142).*

ENGRAVED BY B. T. POUNCY, 1785

photograph (right): *Rydal Water is impossible to photograph from Farington's viewpoint because of plantations of trees. The watercolour (and the engraving) makes Rydal Water and its surroundings more dramatic than they are in reality. This view is from the north end of the lake looking south.*

3 | Lower waterfall, Rydal

'This cascade is seen through the window of the summer house in Sir Michael Fleming's garden at Rydal Hall. There is another fall of the same stream extremely well worth seeing though in a different stile of beauty a little above the house. Public mention was first made of the elegant little scene which is the subject of this plate by Mr Mason, the editor of Mr Gray's letters, nor will the reader be displeased to have an account of it in his own words. "Here nature has performed everything in little that she usually executes on a larger scale; and on that account, like the miniature painter, seems to have finished every part of it in a fluid manner; not a little fragment of rock thrown into the bason, not a single stem of brushwood that starts from its craggy sides but has its pictureque meaning; and the little central stream dashes down a cleft of the darkest coloured stone, produces an effect of light and shadow beautiful beyond description. This little theatrical scene might be painted as large as the original, on a canvas not bigger than those usually dropped in the Opera House."'

watercolour (opposite): *Lower waterfall at Rydal. There is also a sepia sketch of this view in the Yale album (see page 143).*

ENGRAVED BY B. T. POUNCY, 1788

photograph (right): *This photograph is taken from exactly the same viewpoint as Farington's watercolour. A small summer house was built here in 1668 as a place to frame and enjoy the spectacular waterfall. It was restored recently and is one of the country's earliest examples of a 'viewing station'.*

4 | Looking south towards Windermere

'In the progress of this work, some of the features which distinguish the
situation of Rydal have been noticed. The view here presented exhibits another
species of landscape, which will serve to show the great variety which abounds
in this neighbourhood. The traveller on his tour is directed to the waterfall,
passes at the foot of the mountain, and pursues his course by the side of the
lake. A few circumstances of notoriety are habitually recommended; to these
he pays his visit, and leaves the place, supposing himself sufficiently acquainted
with what is remarkable – But a true idea of the beauties of such a country can
only be formed by him who has time to explore the various elevations, who
considers the different points of view, and suffers no accidental circumstance
to escape him. In this view, which was taken a little above Rydal Hall, part of
Windermere lake, bounded on the west side by Furness Fells, has a beautiful
effect, over the dark umbrage that decorates the hills adjacent to Ambleside,
the situation of which is marked by a few houses in the middle distance.'

watercolour (opposite):
Above Rydal Mount looking south towards Windermere.

ENGRAVED BY B.T. POUNCY, 1789

photograph (right): *This photograph was taken a little above Rydal Hall and to the north-west. The viewpoint is higher up than Farington's in order to avoid the trees in the foreground that now obscure the original view.*

5 | Rydal Bridge

'The scene here represented includes part of the village of Rydal, and is one
of the features in the neighbourhood of Ambleside, which may contribute
to justify the description we gave of its environs. Were a person of leisure to
attend to the various picturesque situations he would meet with, he [would
acknowledge that] the subjects we have selected are not single instances, but
are to be considered only as specimens of the style of the country. The bridge,
which is thrown over the river Rothay, is happily situated in this view; and,
with the group of little cottages near it, forms a beautiful contrast to Rydal
Fell, which rising in alpine grandeur, overshadows the vale.'

watercolour (opposite):
Rydal Bridge and the village of Rydal with Rydal Fell in the background. This bridge and the track over it do not appear on Clarke's map.

ENGRAVED BY W. BYRNE & J. LANDSEER, 1789

photograph (right): *This bridge carries the lane off the Ambleside–Rydal road which runs beneath Loughrigg Fell following the river Rothay. The group of buildings seen through the trees is in the same position as the cottages in the watercolour and engraving with Rydal Fell in the background.*

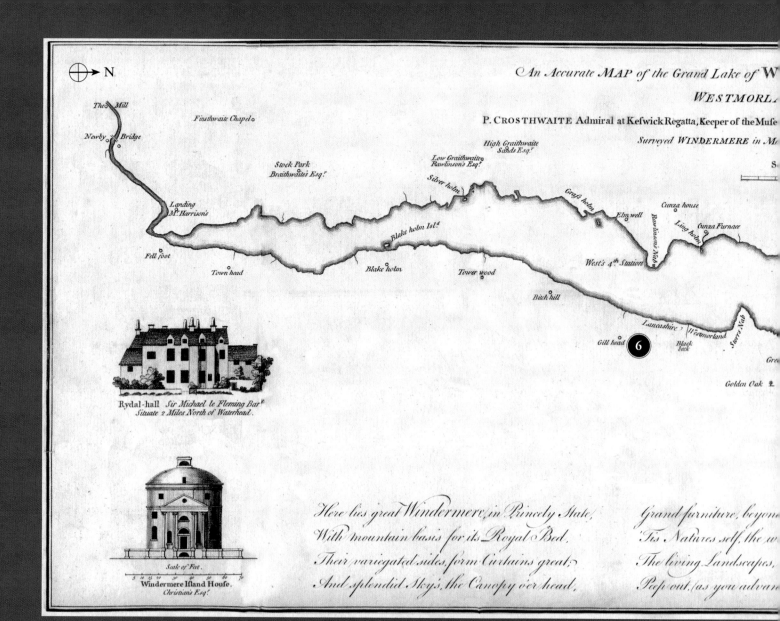

An Accurate MAP of the Grand Lake of W

WESTMORLA

P. CROSTHWAITE Admiral at Kefwick Regatta, Keeper of the Mufe

Surveyed WINDERMERE in Mo

S

The Mill

Finsthwaite Chapel

Newby Bridge

High Graithwaite Sands Esqr

Stock Park Braithwaite's Esqr

Low Graithwaite Rawlinson's Esqr

Landing Mr Harrison's

Silver holm

Grafs holm

Cunza house

Elm well

Ling holm

Cunza Furnace

Fell foot

Blake holm Isl^d

West's 4th Station

Town head

Blake holm

Tower wood

Birch hill

Lancashire Westmorland

Storrs Nab

Gill head **6**

Black beck

Gre

Golden Oak

Rydal-hall Sir Michael le Fleming Bar^t
Situate 2 Miles North of Waterhead.

Scale of Feet.
Windermere Ifland House.
Christian's Esqr

Here lies great Windermere, in Princely State,
With mountain basis for its Royal Bed.
Their variegated sides, form Curtains great,
And splendid Sky's, the Canopy o'er head,

Grand furniture, beyon
'Tis Natures self, the w
The living Landscapes,
Peep out (as you advan

Windermere

1. Stock-Gill Force, Ambleside
2. The road from Clappergate to Ambleside
3. Brathay Bridge, near Ambleside
4. Windermere from above Rayrigg
5. Windermere from the west shore
6. Windermere from Gill Head

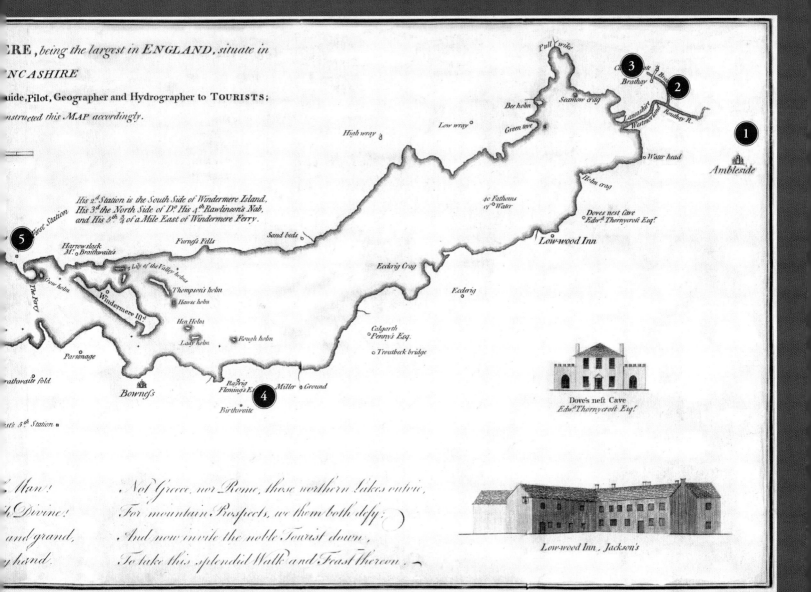

ERE , *being the largest in* ENGLAND, *situate in*

NCASHIRE

uide, Pilot, Geographer and Hydrographer *to* TOURISTS;

nstructed this MAP *accordingly.*

3

Ch——nt Br—
Brathay

2

Lancashire
Westmorland   Brathay R.

1

Pull wike

Bee holm   Seathw crag

Low wray   Green tove

High wray   Water head

Ambleside

His 2.ª Station is the South Side of Windermere Island.
His 3.ª the North Side of D.º His 4.ᵗʰ Rawlinson's Nab,
and His 5.ᵗʰ ¾ of a Mile East of Windermere Ferry.

40 Fathoms
of Water

Doves nest Cave
Edwᵈ Thornycroft Esqʳ

5 First Station

Holm crag

Low-wood Inn

Harrow slack
Mʳ Braithwaite's

Furness Fells   Sand beds

Crow holm

Lily of the Valley holms

The Ferry

Thompson's holm

Windermere Isᵈ

Hawse holm

Ecclerig Crag

Hen Holm

Rough holm

Lady holm

Ecclerig

Parsonage

Calgarth
Penny's Esq.

aithwaite fold

Bownefs

Rayrig
Fleming's Eʳ   Miller   Ground

Troutbeck bridge

4

Birthwaite

Dove's nest Cave
Edwᵈ Thornycroft Esqʳ

st's 5ᵗʰ Station ■

Low-wood Inn , Jackson's

Man!   Not Greece, nor Rome, those northern Lakes outvie,

Divine!   For mountain Prospects, we them both defy:

and grand,   And now invite the noble Tourist down,

hand.   To take this splendid Walk and Feast thereon.

ENGRAVED BY S. MIDDIMAN, 1816

1 | Stock-Gill Force, Ambleside

'At the distance of nearly a mile from the Salutation Inn, at Ambleside, is Stock-Gill Force, a grand cascade, which, for its singular beauty, may almost be considered as a rival of the far-famed water-fall of Lowdore, near Keswick. Passing the Inn yard, we ascend a steep road, and, entering a copse, proceeded towards the Force. Long before we reached the cataract itself we could distinctly hear the thundering echo of the rushing water. The gill or torrent which supplies the cascade, takes its rise in the mountains behind Ambleside, and flows in a narrow channel through an opening of rocks, partially concealed by overhanging trees. Having reached the station which appears in the right foreground on the engraving, we looked upwards to the height

engraving (above): *There is no Farington watercolour or sketch of these falls in the Yale album, nor an engraving in the 1789 volume. Gray passed just below them but did not visit them. It is interesting to see how little they have changed. The ledge on which the man stands is still there.*

of about three hundred feet. The torrent flows in two distinct streams, separated by a rocky yet verdant island, about forty feet wide, covered with moss and shrubs, and foaming with tremendous noise. After falling about one hundred and fifty feet, the streams unite, and are dashed from rock to rock into a dark gulph, unfathomable to the eye, from which it is concealed by some trees that stretch themselves across the basin. Thence the water flows over a rough and craggy channel, through a narrow gill or valley, luxuriantly adorned with rock and wood; and after forming two or three other pretty cascades, each of which would furnish a pleasing study to the artist, it falls into the Rothay, a little below Ambleside.' TH

2 | The road from Clappergate to Ambleside

'Ambleside is situated on the swift decline of a hill, over which many high mountains rise towards the north. In Camden's time, various ruins of the ancient Amboglana of the Romans were to be seen here. Near the head of Windermere, and at a little distance from the point where this view was taken, is the vestige of a Roman station. It lies in a meadow on a level with the lake, and as supposed, was called the Dictis, where part of the cohort of the numerous Nerviorum Dictentium was stationed. The extent of the fortress, as he gives dimensions, was one hundred and thirty-two ells in length and eighty in breadth. In form an oblong square with obtuse angles. It is placed near the meeting of all the roads from Penrith, Keswick, Ravensglass, Furness and Kendal, which it commanded, and was accessible only on one side. Roman bricks, urns, and other earthern vessels, coins, mill-stones or quern-stones, as he calls them, were frequently found here. The natural beauties of this part of the country are of very superior order. It would scarcely be partial to say that a greater variety of romantic and picturesque scenery is to be found in the neighbourhood of Ambleside, than can be met in any other part of this interesting country within the same compass.'

watercolour (opposite): *View of Ambleside across the Rothay River that runs behind the trees at the bottom of the field.*

ENGRAVED BY T. MEDLAND, 1789

photograph (right): *It was astonishing to find a position, close to Farington's viewpoint from which to photograph this view, as Ambleside has greatly expanded since Farington's day. Unfortunately the bridge and the river are obscured by trees. The bridge is just at the bottom of the field where a car can be seen. The road to Clappergate and Brathay Bridge running up the left of the field follows the route of the lane in the watercolour and engraving. The roofs of Ambleside can also be glimpsed. The river flows along the bottom of the field behind the trees. The mountains in the distance are clearly those in the watercolour and engraving.*

3 | Brathay Bridge, near Ambleside

'It has already been remarked that this country derives no inconsiderable advantage in respect of beauty from its buildings and bridges. The present view is selected pricipally with a design of illustrating and confirming that observation. The scene itself lies upon the road leading from Ambleside to Hawkshead about a mile from the former place. It can hardly fail to attract the notice of the admirer of landscape and has not unfrequently called into exercise the powers of the artist. The long lines and flat roofs so much admired in the Italian buildings are peculiarly striking. The houses form a part of the village of Clappersgate. Lancashire is separated from Westmorland by the Brathay: It soon unites itself with the Rothay, and after a short course they enter Windermere together. The upper part of the hill remains clear while its skirts are obscured by a cloud. This effect, though common enough among mountains, appears curious to those who have been accustomed only to level land.'

watercolour (left): *Brathay Bridge over the river Brathay.. There is a sepia sketch of this view but instead of a man leading a horse off the bridge and figures on the road behind, there are simply three characters on the right approaching the bridge (see page 144).*

ENGRAVED BY W. BYRNE & T. MEDLAND, 1787

photograph (right): *By choosing a moment before the leaves came out, it was possible to photograph the bridge with the houses of Clappergate visible through the branches and Todd Crag behind. The river Brathay passes beneath this bridge and about half a mile further on joins the Rothay, which flows into Windermere.*

4 | Windermere from above Rayrigg

'This view comprehends the lower reach of Windermere looking towards the south, and is the reverse of that given from Gill-Head. The lake here assumes the appearance of a noble river, indented with wooded peninsulas intersecting each other: at the distance of several miles, it narrows into a stream of a moderate width, which passing by the village of Newby soon enters an arm of the sea. Rarig, which lies below, is placed near the road leading from Bowness to Ambleside, and is a situation much admired for the many beautiful points of view which are found in its vicinity.'

watercolour (opposite): *View from above Rayrigg south across Windermere. The two men (one on horseback) and a dog are replaced in the engraving by a figure on horseback driving two cows. There is also a sepia sketch of this same scene showing two mounted horsemen with a figure sitting on the bank (see page 144).*

ENGRAVED BY W. BYRNE & T. MEDLAND, 1789

photograph (right): *Once again it was impossible to find Farington's view because of trees. It is possible that this view is from the edge of the mound in the centre of Farington's watercolour. Rayrigg Hall is at the other side of the further field, just visible amongst the trees.*

5 | Windermere from the west shore

'The views given of Windermere, when compared with each other, show that the style of that lake and its environs differs materially from the other lakes which are exhibited in the course of this work. That it is a landscape of a softer species, and wears a more cultivated appearance. In grandeur and sublimity it is inferior to Derwentwater and Ullswater; but excells both in splendour and extent. Each lake has a peculiar and striking character; the difficulty, therefore, with the artist, is to determine on those situations where the distinction is marked in the strongest manner. The islands on Windermere (if they may be so called, many of them being rather wooded rocks), are ten in number, composing a kind of archipelago, and in some views appearing to separate the upper from the lower reach of the lake. In this view, which was taken on the western side, nearly opposite the village of Bowness, the Great Island, which contains about thirty acres, forms a principal object. It is of oblong shape, traversing the lake in an oblique line, and is the only one on which a building is erected. From Ferry House beneath Bowness, is the great pass of communication from the western to eastern shore.'

watercolour (left): *Windermere looking north-east over the Great Island (Belle Isle) from the west shore. The island is portrayed here by adopting Gilpin's picturesque rules.*

engraving (right): *In the watercolour the central figure with the stick and bundle over his shoulder has his back to us. In the engraving he is coming towards us.*

ENGRAVED BY W. BYRNE & J. LANDSEER, 1789

photograph (right): *Early on Windermere became the most popular of the lakes and from the mid-nineteenth century was accessible by railway. Many industrialists from the north and the Midlands built houses on its shores with large plantations of firs and other evergreens. These trees now obscure many of the views painted by eighteenth- and early nineteenth-century artists. Here Farington seems to have reduced the size of Great Island (Belle Isle), as did many artists, to make his lake scenes more picturesque. This photograph should have been taken from West's 'station', marked on Crosthwaite's map, but unfortunately trees now obscure the view.*

6 | Windermere from Gill Head

'Windermere or Winandermere as it is sometimes called, is the largest of the lakes, extending from north to south upwards of ten miles. In breadth it rarely exceeds one, and narrows considerably towards the lower end. The northern and western coasts are wild and mountainous, the eastern and southern are more depressed, being in some parts cultivated, in others woody. At about an equal distance from each extremity stands the village of Bowness. Opposite to it the lake is divided into two parts by a cluster of islands, one of which, being much larger than the rest is usually called Great Island. The drawing of this subject was made near a place called Gill-Head, about three miles below Bowness. It comprehends a general view of the lake looking towards the north. The accompanyments of this lake are highly beautiful, and its extent gives an air of great magnificence.'

watercolour (opposite): *view looking north up Windermere towards Ambleside. Farington's foreground is as picturesque as ever.*

ENGRAVED BY T. MEDLAND, 1788

photograph (right): *Farington's view from Gill Head is no longer possible to photograph because of trees but this photograph was taken from a hill a little to the north that rises above the surrounding trees and offers a very similar view.*

PART FIVE

Additional Drawings

The following pages include additional watercolours, sepia sketches
and pen-and-ink washes from the Yale album relating to Gray's tour and
a few engravings from the 1816 volume that also relate to it. In addition
there is one watercolour that does not relate to Gray's tour but which has
been included so that this book is a complete record of the Yale album.

North entrance to Keswick (left): *This sepia sketch, unlike the watercolour on page 82, has washerwomen on the near side of the river, and only one man and a dog walking towards the bridge and no people on the bridge.*

Ullswater (below): *This watercolour was not engraved for the 1789 or 1816 volumes. It is a view north-east down Ullswater from some way up Hallin Fell with Dunmallet Hill in the distance.*

Derwentwater and the Vale of Keswick (right): *see page 90.*

Patterdale from Martindale Fell (below): *A sepia sketch of the same scene as that on page 68 but here there are no figures.*

Lodore Falls (top left): *from the same viewpoint as that of the watercolour above.*

Lodore Falls (middle left): *a similar view to that of the main watercolour on page 88.*

'Ullswater: Col. Robinson's' (bottom left): *The lower reach of Ullswater from above Pooley (see the sepia sketch on page 74).*

Lodore Falls (above): *from a different viewpoint to that of the main watercolour on page 88. There is no engraving of this view in the 1789 or 1816 volumes*

Grange in Borrowdale (above): *engraving from the 1816 volume.*

Grange in Borrowdale (opposite top): *a similar view to that of the watercolour on page 96.*

Grasmere (opposite bottom left): *possibly a sketch in preparation for the engraving in the 1816 volume (see page 110).*

View from Six-mile-stone (opposite bottom right): *sketch of a similar view to the watercolour on page 104.*

Rydal Water (above): *a similar view to that of the watercolour on page 112 but with figures on horseback on the track instead of sheep.*

Rydal Water (left): *the engraving from the 1816 volume but with two figures coming up the track.*

**Lower waterfall at Rydal
(above):** *pen-and-ink wash
of the same view as that of the
watercolour on page 114.*

**Looking towards Ambleside
up the river Rothay (right):**
*There is no engraving of this
view in either the 1789 or the
1816 volumes.*

Brathay Bridge (opposite top): *pen-and-ink wash of the same view as that of the watercolour (see page 126).*

Gordale Scar (right): *Gray visited Gordale Scar on 13 October after leaving the lakes behind him. There is no watercolour of this in the Yale album, only this sepia sketch. Nor is there an engraving of it in either the 1789 or the 1816 volumes (see page 48, where he mentions it in his journal).*

Unidentified landscape (right): *possibly the Head of Windermere.*

View of Windermere from above Rayrigg looking south (opposite bottom right): *pen-and-ink wash of the same view as that of the watercolour on page 128.*

Nunnery in Cumberland (opposite bottom left): *there is an engraving of this scene in the 1816 volume but Gray did not visit these falls on his 1769 tour. This has been included as it appears in the Yale album and by including it, this book reproduces the complete album.*

PART SIX

Sample Pages from the Manuscript of the Journal of Thomas Gray's Tour of the Lakes of 1769 in the John Murray Collection

CUMBERLAND,
WESTMORLAND,
LANCASHIRE,
AND
YORKSHIRE.
1769.

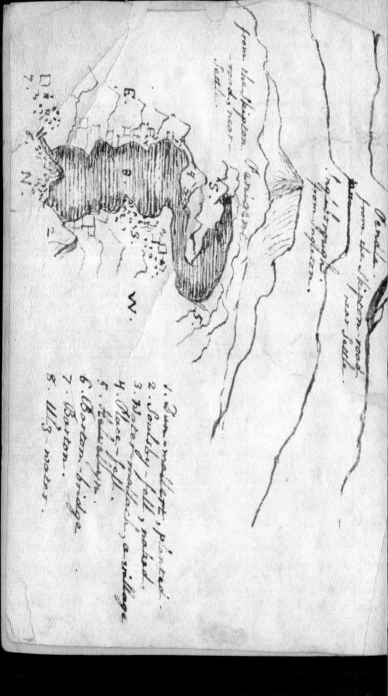

...[at] Keswick learn'd, that the turnpike road from thence over Whinlatter-fall extends no farther than thro' Cocker-mouth & Whitehaven X to Egremont, & there ends X vide infra. 23-3

That the way along the east-side of Bassingthwaite, or Low-water (w.ch is 8 miles) to Ews-bridge over Darwent is made in part only, about 3 miles of it being a cart-road slippery & dangerous, or else narrow & stony lane. the new road from Cockermouth is made (5 miles) to Ews-bridge, & now carrying on towards Penrith.

That the way from Keswick to Amble-side (18 m:) is turnpike not yet com-pleated by about 3 miles. the unmade way is thro' narrow country lanes, or rocky road, but nothing dangerous by day-light. it runs mostly thro' deep romantic vallies by the waters of Wi-born at the foot of Helvellyn-Fell, by Grasmere & Ridall. Ambleside is a little Market-town, but the inns are too mean & unfrequented to lie at. from thence to Kendal is 14 miles, turnpike-road, but not quite finish'd. it goes near 5 m: on the side of Wi-nander-water with beautiful views, mostly up hill, but good road, except a small part not yet compleated, & -

this is very safe.

From Kendal there is a fine turn
=pike lately made to Ulverston (or
Ouston) in Furness. it goes by the fo
of Winander-mere-water & over
Penny-bridge avoiding all the se
·sands, & with many uncommon
views the whole way.

There is also a road not quit
finish'd to Kirby-Lonsdale. from
thence it is compleated by Ingle
to Settle in Yorkshire, excellent ry

There is also a turnpike, tha
goes by Sedbargh & over Cam-
to Ashrig in Wensledale.

x I learn'd at Kendal, that the Ul
=ston-turnpike is continued a few
miles to Dalton, & there ends: but the
a branch of it (not quite compleat
goes off into Cumberland to Ravengl
& so on along the coast to Egremon
in this part of it, a sand must necessarily
pass'd, but it is only 3 or 400 yard
over, & very safe.

Journal continued from Keswick.
Oct: 8. Sun. Bid farewell to Keswick, & took the
Ambleside-road in a gloomy morning.
S, & E: & afterwards N:E:. about 2 m:
from the Town mounted an eminence
call'd Castle-rig, & the sun breaking-
out discover'd the most beautiful-
view I have yet seen of the whole
valley behind me, the two Lakes, the
river, & all the mountains. I had
almost a mind to have gone back
again.
The road in some little patches is
not compleated yet, but good country
road thro' a few narrow & stony-
lanes, very safe in broad day-light.
this is the case about Causeway-foot
& among Naddle-Fells to Lancrait
the vale you go in has little breadth
the mountains are vast & rocky, the-
fields little & poor, & the inhabitant
are now making hay, & see not the sun by two hours in a
day so long as at Keswick.
Came to the foot of Halvellyn, a-
long wth an excellent road is carried, looking down from a little height
on Lec's-water (call'd also Thirlmere
or Wiborn-water) &, soon descending on
it's margin, the water looks black

from its depth (tho' really clear as
glass) & from the gloom of the vast
crags, that scowl over it. it is narr
& about 3 m:long, resembling a
river in its course. little shining
torrents hurry down the rocks
join it, but not a bush to overs=
=dow them, or cover their march
all is rock & loose stones up to
the very brow, w:th is so near
your way, that not, above half the
height of Helvellyn can be seen.

Past by the little Chappel of
Wiborn, out of w:ch the Sunday-c
=gregation were then issuing.

Past a beck near Dunmail-
-raise, & enter'd Westmoreland
a second time. now begin to see
Helm-Crag distinguish'd from its
rugged neighbours not so much by
it's height, as by the strange broke
outline of its top, like some giga
=tic building demolish'd, & the ston
that composed it, flung cross eac
other in wild confusion. just be
=yond it opens one of the sweete
landscapes, that art ever attempte

imitate. ~~its Grasmere water~~ (the
~~com of y~~ in mountains ~~spreading~~
~~opening~~ here into a broad
~~bason~~) discovers in the midst Grasmere
water. its margin is hollow'd into small
bays, with bold eminences some of
rock, some of soft turf, that ~~elevate~~ half con:
ceal, the figure
vary, the little lake they command,
from the shore a low promontory
pushes itself far into the water, &
on it stands a white village with the
parish-church rising in the midst of
it, hanging enclosures, corn-fields
& meadows
green as an emerald, with their trees
& hedges & cattle fill up the whole
space from the edge of the water &
just opposite to you, is a large farm-
house at the bottom of a steep
smooth ~~lawn~~ embosom'd in old woods,
which climb half way up the mountain's side, & discover above them
a ~~wall of~~ broken line of crags, that
crown the scene. not a single red
tile, no flaring Gentleman's house,
or garden walls, break in upon the
repose of this little unsuspected paradise,
but all is peace, happy
rusticity & poverty in its neatest
most becoming attire.
The road winds here over Grasmere
hill, whose rocks soon conceal the
water from your sight, yet it continues

Select Bibliography

Andrews, Malcolm. *The Search for the Picturesque*. Scolar Press, 1989

Bricknell, Peter (ed.). *The Illustrated Wordsworth Guide to the Lakes*. Select Editions, 1984

Clarke, James. *A Survey of the Lakes of Cumberland, Westmorland & Lancashire*. Second edition, London, 1789.

Daiches, David and Flower, John. *Literary Landscapes of the British Isles*. Paddington Press, 1979

Farington, Joseph. *Diary of Joseph Farington (1793–1821)*. 16 vols. Yale University Press, 1978–84. Index volume by Evelyn Newby. 1998

Farington, Joseph. *Views of the Lakes etc. in Cumberland and Westmorland. Engraved from drawings made by Joseph Farington R.A.* Published by William Byrne, London, 1789

Farington, Joseph. *The Lakes of Lancashire, Westmorland and Cumberland: Delineated in forty-three engravings from drawings by Joseph Farington R.A. With descriptions Historical, Topographical and Picturesque. The result of a tour made in the summer of 1816.* By Thomas Hartwell Horne. T. Cadell & W. Davies, London, 1816

Gilpin, William. *Observations on Several Parts of England, particularly the Mountains & Lakes of Cumberland & Westmoreland, relative chiefly to Picturesque Beauty, made in the Year 1772*. 2 vols. Third edition, London, 1808

Gilpin, William. *Observations relative chiefly to Picturesque Beauty made in the year 1776 of Several Parts of Great Britain; particularly the High-lands of Scotland. 2 vols.* London, 1789

Gilpin, William and Mason, William. MSS correspondence between William Gilpin and William Mason, 1772–97. Bodleian Library

Gilpin, William. Manuscript notebooks of his Tour through England, 1772. 8 vols. Bodleian Library.

Gray, Thomas. *Thomas Gray's Journal of his Visit to the Lake District in October 1769*. Transcribed and edited by William Roberts. Liverpool University Press, 2001

Gray, Thomas. *Notes on a Tour through France and Italy undertaken in the years 1739 to 1741*. Transcribed and edited by William Roberts. Carlisle, 2003

Gray, Thomas. *Correspondence of Thomas Gray.* Edited by Paget Toynbee and Leonard Whibley. 3 vols. Clarendon Press, 1935

Gray, Thomas. *The Traveller's Companion in a Tour through England and Wales containing a catalogue of the Antiquities etc. arranged by the Late Mr Gray.* New edition. London, 1789

Hargreaves, Matthew. *Great British Watercolours from the Paul Mellon Collection.* Yale Center for British Art, 2007

Hebron, Stephen, Shields, Conan and Wilcox, Timothy. *The Solitude of the Mountains: Constable and the Lake District.* The Wordsworth Trust, 2006

Hebron, Stephen. *In the Line of Beauty: Early Views of the Lake District by Amateur Artists.* The Wordsworth Trust, 2008

Ketton-Cremer, R.W. *Thomas Gray: A Biography.* Cambridge University Press, 1955

Murray's Hand-Book to the Lakes: Westmorland and Cumberland. John Murray, 1889

Nicholson, Norman. *The Lakers: the First Tourists.* Robert Hale, 1955

Otley, Jonathan. *A Concise Description of the English Lakes and Adjacent Mountains with General Direction to Tourists.* Fifth edition. London, 1833

Ousby, Ian. *Englishman's England.* Cambridge University Press, 1990

Parris, Leslie. *Landscape in Britain c.1750–1850.* The Tate Gallery, 1973

Powell, Cecilia and Hebron, Stephen. *Savage Grandeur and Noblest Thoughts: Discovering the Lake District 1750–1820.* The Wordsworth Trust, 2010

Thompson, Ian. *The English Lakes: A History.* Bloomsbury, 2010

Tyler, Ian. *Thirlmere Mines and the Drowning of the Valley.* Blue Rock Publications, 2005

West, Thomas. *A Guide to the Lakes in Cumberland, Westmorland and Lancashire.* Third edition. London, 1784

Wordsworth, Jonathan, Jaye, Michael C. and Woof, Robert. *William Wordsworth and the Age of English Romanticism.* The Wordsworth Trust, 1987